Dynamics of Writing

Sara Miller McCune founded SAGE Publishing in 1965 to support the dissemination of usable knowledge and educate a global community. SAGE publishes more than 1000 journals and over 800 new books each year, spanning a wide range of subject areas. Our growing selection of library products includes archives, data, case studies and video. SAGE remains majority owned by our founder and after her lifetime will become owned by a charitable trust that secures the company's continued independence.

Los Angeles | London | New Delhi | Singapore | Washington DC | Melbourne

Dynamics of Writing

An Exercise Guide

Vincent F. Filak
University of Wisconsin–Oshkosh

FOR INFORMATION:

CQ Press
2455 Teller Road
Thousand Oaks, California 91320
E-mail: order@sagepub.com

SAGE Publications Ltd.
1 Oliver's Yard
55 City Road
London EC1Y 1SP
United Kingdom

SAGE Publications India Pvt. Ltd.
B 1/I 1 Mohan Cooperative Industrial Area
Mathura Road, New Delhi 110 044
India

SAGE Publications Asia-Pacific Pte. Ltd.
3 Church Street
#10-04 Samsung Hub
Singapore 049483

Printed in the United States of America

Library of Congress Cataloging-in-Publication Data

Names: Filak, Vincent F., author.

Title: Dynamics of writing : an exercise guide / Vincent F. Filak.

Description: Los Angeles : CQ Press, [2019]

Identifiers: LCCN 2017038396 | ISBN 9781506347660 (pbk. : acid-free paper)

Subjects: LCSH: Journalism—Handbooks, manuals, etc. | Journalism—Authorship—Handbooks, manuals, etc. | Online journalism—Handbooks, manuals, etc. | Online journalism—Authorship—Handbooks, manuals, etc.

Classification: LCC PN4775 .F455 2019 | DDC 808.06/607—dc23
LC record available at https://lccn.loc.gov/2017038396

This book is printed on acid-free paper.

Acquisitions Editor: Terri Accomazzo
Content Development Editor: Anna Villarruel
Editorial Assistant: Erik Helton
Production Editor: Bennie Clark Allen
Copy Editor: Jim Kelly
Typesetter: C&M Digitals (P) Ltd.
Proofreader: Jen Grubba
Cover Designer: Scott Van Atta
Marketing Manager: Jillian Oelson

18 19 20 21 22 10 9 8 7 6 5 4 3 2 1

TABLE OF CONTENTS

AUDIENCE-CENTRIC JOURNALISM

REVIEW

1. What is audience-centric journalism? How is it similar to what traditional media outlets have done in years past, and how is it different?

2. This chapter noted that generations of journalists were previously taught in "silos" based on the fields they saw themselves entering. What does this mean?

3. Define and differentiate between audience "wants" and audience "needs" when it comes to a media diet. How does the book say you should balance these topics as a journalist?

4. Define and differentiate among the three ways in which the book states you should break down an audience: demographic information, psychographic information and geographic information.

5. What do the letters in the acronym "FOCII" stand for, and what does it mean overall as a concept?

WRITING EXERCISES

1. Give an example of a piece of infotainment and explain how it integrates knowledge and entertainment to reach an audience.

2. Find a story on the web that you believe to be "fake news" and analyze it.
    *   Use sources you believe to be credible, or sources your instructor considers credible, to demonstrate the falsity of the story's claims.
    *   Explain why you think the story does or doesn't fully fit the definition of "fake news."
    *   Also, explain why you think the story attracts readers, despite its factual inaccuracies.

3. Keep a running list of the media sources you use in one day.
    *   Note each platform on which you consume the information. For example, you might note that you read a print copy of the student newspaper, but you watched a national television station on your smartphone.
    *   Where do you get the most information, and which outlets listed in the chapter don't you use?
    *   Also, see if you can detect a pattern in your information consumption habits with regard to platforms you use and sources you visit.

4. Select one source of information you found to be dominating your media diet and examine it for the three things the book says journalists "owe" their audience: accuracy, value and fairness/objectivity. How well do you think this source does in meeting those standards? In what areas does the source excel, and where could it do a better job for its readers?

5. Read the comments on an article that interests you.
    *   Keep track of how many initial responses are made to the article as well as how many posts are made in direct response to comments by other posters.

- How many people participated in this conversation, and does any particular person dominate the discussion?
- Does this discussion add to the overall value of the story itself?
- Do you find particular merit or value in any one train of thought? Cite examples to justify your opinion.

6. Read each of the following sentences and explain which interest elements most directly apply to it and why:

   - President Donald Trump and First Lady Melania Trump announced today that they are getting a divorce, marking the first time a sitting president has faced this situation.
   - The Board of Trustees at your school announced last week that it will increase tuition by 10 percent next year, despite your school president's specific request to cut tuition costs.
   - City officials announced today that researchers found that a rare form of an airborne disease has infected at least three people in your town.

7. Review a week's worth of coverage in a local media outlet (newspaper, website, TV station, etc.) and keep track of the topics they cover and which kinds of news get the most attention. Review your notes and write a short paper that explains your findings and if you think the coverage reflects the interests of the audience of the media outlet.

CRITICAL THINKING

REVIEW

1. Define critical thinking and give an example of critical versus uncritical thinking.

2. Define and differentiate between learning and thinking.

3. What are the four things the book notes are the signs of a good critical thinker?

4. The chapter notes that you should "avoid self-importance." What does that mean, and how does the chapter suggest you do this?

WRITING EXERCISES

1. Find a story in a local or student news publication and apply the Topeka Test to it.
   - Does the story pass the test?
   - Is there enough background information or vital context to make sense for the reader?

- If you think it would fail the test, what would you include to improve it and make it a more reader-friendly story?

2. Check out multiple online sources, such as CNN.com, FoxNews.com and MSNBC .com, for their coverage of a topic of current interest. Apply the standard of open-minded thinking to the story each outlet has written regarding that topic. Do you see active critical thinking from each of these outlets? Does inherent bias come forth in the writing?

3. Review a transcript of a White House press briefing that includes a question-and-answer session. Examine each question the reporters ask and analyze the purpose of these questions, based on the discussion of questions in this chapter.

   - Does the question have value?
   - Is the reporter showing off?
   - Will the answer help the reporter's audience?
   - Does the reporter appear informed on the topic?
   - Does the question reflect any aspect of critical thinking?

4. Pick up a supermarket tabloid or an entertainment magazine that focuses on celebrity news. Review the content and assess to what degree the information in here is "fast food news."

   - What are the stories in this publication really telling readers?
   - To what degree is this information valuable to readers?
   - Do any of the pieces include critical thinking or require deeper analysis from readers?

5. Pick a story in a local or student news publication and read it from a critical-thinking perspective. When you are finished, list five questions you think need to be more deeply explored in the story or remain unanswered by the author. Then, outline the sources you would interview to answer those questions.

BASICS OF WRITING

REVIEW

1. What does your book say are the two most important questions you should consider when you decide how to structure your story?

2. The book suggests building a lead from the inside out. What are the two or three key elements that should be at the core of a good lead sentence?

3. Define and differentiate between a name-recognition lead and an interesting-action lead. How does each lead work, and when is it most appropriate to use each lead?

4. How should you order information in your story if you are using the inverted-pyramid format?

5. According to the book, how long should most of your paragraphs be in a standard inverted-pyramid story?

6. Define and differentiate between a direct quote and an indirect quote (also known as paraphrase). What is the purpose and value of each form of quoting? When is it best to use each kind of quote?

7. What is an attribution, and how does it help you as a journalist?

8. What is the preferred verb of attribution? What other verbs of attribution are acceptable, and under what circumstances are those verbs acceptable?

WRITING EXERCISES

1. Read each of the following sentences and boil them down to a simple noun-verb-object structure (who did what to whom or what). Feel free to use words you don't find in the sentence, particularly if you want to use a stronger verb or a more concrete noun.

   a. By a 5-0 vote, the Wilton School Board decided Monday to not renew the contract of Wilton High School Principal Layne Sorvo, after he was accused of misconduct over the past year.

   b. Wesley Nimford, the creator of a multimillion-dollar time management app, said he will likely consider several new ventures but is most interested in a run for president.

   c. The Milsmith Owls scored two defensive touchdowns, rushed for three more and scored on a final-play two-point conversion to defeat the rival Oxbow Foxes, 43-42, on Friday.

   d. The Campus Herald, the student newspaper at North Central College, is being accused of libel in a court filing by a professor who was falsely accused in the paper of taking money for grades.

2. **EVENT-LEAD PRACTICE**

   Use each of these chunks of text to create a solid event lead that has a sharp focus and avoids drawing attention to the event itself:

   a. Facebook founder and CEO Mark Zuckerberg gave a speech to the annual Facebook developers conference today. He laid out his vision for the next 10 years of social media and explained that he saw video as vital. Zuckerberg said that video will connect all people, not just the wealthiest people, to all the opportunities of the internet. He compared the importance of video in 10 years in terms of content sharing and connectivity to the way mobile communication became essential over the previous 10 years. The company's goal with video is to give everyone everywhere the ability to share anything they want with anyone else.

   b. The Board of Trustees at Northwest Central State College met Tuesday to discuss several key issues. The main issue on the table was the cost of education and how it affects the quality of education. With diminishing state funds, the school was losing many faculty members from key areas of research and teaching. The school also had to eliminate several classes because it lacked the resources to teach them. The board agreed to raise tuition this year by 3 percent to improve course offerings and raise it another 3 percent next year to offer pay increases to faculty. The board passed this plan by a 9-0 vote.

   c. Jacoby Everson, the chancellor of Eastern State University, held a press conference today to announce some changes to the institution. He said he remembered being a new faculty member on campus almost 40 years ago, and he marveled at how much the university has grown in that time. He mentioned that his past 20 years, when he has served as chancellor, have been among the happiest of his life. However, he wanted to make a change in life, so at the end of this year, he will be retiring.

3. **LEAD-REWRITING PRACTICE**

   Below are several problematic leads. Rewrite them to eliminate the specific problem associated with each lead and to improve their overall readability:

   a. You should attend the 4 p.m. pep rally Friday outside Memorial Stadium for our Eastern High School team as they prepare for the annual rivalry game against Western High School.

b. Have you ever wondered what it would be like to find buried treasure? Archeology professor Harold Smith figures everyone has at one point, which is why he converted his summer class into a study-abroad opportunity to search for missing valuables at a former pirate stronghold along the Barbary Coast.

c. Everybody has been hungry at one point in class and been without food. This is why Central College student Albert Todello created his "Campus Cravings" app, which connects students who need a snack with his delivery service that will bring granola bars, popcorn or a protein shake right into the classroom.

4. **BRIEF-WRITING PRACTICE**

Use the information below to create a four-paragraph, inverted-pyramid brief. Each paragraph should be one sentence long and should attribute the information to your source. The first sentence is your lead, and the remaining three single-sentence paragraphs should be organized so that information is presented in descending order of importance.

Source: Lt. Carl Wexler, Daytonville Fire Department

INFORMATION: The Daytonville Fire Department deployed Ladder Truck 5, Chief's Car 4, Pumper Truck 11 and additional support vehicles to 121 S. Eighth St. after receiving a 911 call around 5:30 p.m. Tuesday. Firefighters arrived to find the two-story, four-bedroom home fully enveloped in flames. The homeowner, Clarence Combs, was outside of the home, as was his wife, Jane, and their daughter, Zelda. He stated that no one else was left inside. Nobody was injured.

Firefighters deployed several hose lines and fought the blaze for three hours until getting full control of the situation. After the fire was extinguished, two fire marshals investigated the scene and determined that the fire was caused by an overheated dryer in the basement. The fire then spread along the basement's ceiling, which consisted mostly of very old wood. The house was constructed in 1892 and was the oldest home in Daytonville.

The home is considered a total loss, and the loss is estimated to be $300,000 in damages.

5. **SINGLE-SOURCE WRITING PRACTICE**

On page 12 is the transcript of President Donald Trump's inaugural address. Write a simple lead that captures the core of what you think this speech is about (a summary lead or a name-recognition lead would likely be your best approach). Then, write the remainder of the piece in an inverted-pyramid format that follows the paraphrase-quote approach discussed in the chapter. Be sure to attribute the paraphrases and the direct quotes to the source, using the verb "said" in each case. The piece should be no longer than two pages, typed, double-spaced.

6. **MULTIPLE-SOURCE WRITING PRACTICE**

On pages 15 to 24 are the text of President Barack Obama's 2016 State of the Union address and South Carolina Gov. Nikki Haley's official Republican response to it. Read through both speeches and find the core themes being discussed. Then, create an inverted-pyramid piece that starts with a quality lead and relies on a paraphrase-quote structure to tell the remainder of the story. Use paraphrases and quotes, as you did in the previous exercise, but seek balance between the two sources where it is appropriate. The story should be between 2 and 2.5 pages in length.

FOR EXERCISE 5

Remarks of President Donald J. Trump—As Prepared for Delivery

Inaugural Address

Friday, January 20, 2017

Washington, D.C.

Chief Justice Roberts, President Carter, President Clinton, President Bush, President Obama, fellow Americans, and people of the world: thank you.

We, the citizens of America, are now joined in a great national effort to rebuild our country and to restore its promise for all of our people.

Together, we will determine the course of America and the world for years to come.

We will face challenges. We will confront hardships. But we will get the job done.

Every four years, we gather on these steps to carry out the orderly and peaceful transfer of power, and we are grateful to President Obama and First Lady Michelle Obama for their gracious aid throughout this transition. They have been magnificent.

Today's ceremony, however, has very special meaning. Because today we are not merely transferring power from one Administration to another, or from one party to another—but we are transferring power from Washington, D.C. and giving it back to you, the American People.

For too long, a small group in our nation's Capital has reaped the rewards of government while the people have borne the cost.

Washington flourished—but the people did not share in its wealth.

Politicians prospered—but the jobs left, and the factories closed.

The establishment protected itself, but not the citizens of our country.

Their victories have not been your victories; their triumphs have not been your triumphs; and while they celebrated in our nation's Capital, there was little to celebrate for struggling families all across our land.

That all changes—starting right here, and right now, because this moment is your moment: it belongs to you.

It belongs to everyone gathered here today and everyone watching all across America.

This is your day. This is your celebration.

And this, the United States of America, is your country.

What truly matters is not which party controls our government, but whether our government is controlled by the people.

January 20th 2017, will be remembered as the day the people became the rulers of this nation again.

The forgotten men and women of our country will be forgotten no longer.

Everyone is listening to you now.

You came by the tens of millions to become part of a historic movement the likes of which the world has never seen before.

At the center of this movement is a crucial conviction: that a nation exists to serve its citizens.

Americans want great schools for their children, safe neighborhoods for their families, and good jobs for themselves.

These are the just and reasonable demands of a righteous public.

But for too many of our citizens, a different reality exists: Mothers and children trapped in poverty in our inner cities; rusted-out factories scattered like tombstones across the landscape of our nation; an education system, flush with cash, but which leaves our young and beautiful students deprived of knowledge; and the crime and gangs and drugs that have stolen too many lives and robbed our country of so much unrealized potential.

This American carnage stops right here and stops right now.

We are one nation—and their pain is our pain. Their dreams are our dreams; and their success will be our success. We share one heart, one home, and one glorious destiny.

The oath of office I take today is an oath of allegiance to all Americans.

For many decades, we've enriched foreign industry at the expense of American industry;

Subsidized the armies of other countries while allowing for the very sad depletion of our military;

We've defended other nation's borders while refusing to defend our own;

And spent trillions of dollars overseas while America's infrastructure has fallen into disrepair and decay.

We've made other countries rich while the wealth, strength, and confidence of our country has disappeared over the horizon.

One by one, the factories shuttered and left our shores, with not even a thought about the millions upon millions of American workers left behind.

The wealth of our middle class has been ripped from their homes and then redistributed across the entire world.

But that is the past. And now we are looking only to the future.

We assembled here today are issuing a new decree to be heard in every city, in every foreign capital, and in every hall of power.

From this day forward, a new vision will govern our land.

From this moment on, it's going to be America First.

Every decision on trade, on taxes, on immigration, on foreign affairs, will be made to benefit American workers and American families.

We must protect our borders from the ravages of other countries making our products, stealing our companies, and destroying our jobs. Protection will lead to great prosperity and strength.

I will fight for you with every breath in my body—and I will never, ever let you down.

America will start winning again, winning like never before.

We will bring back our jobs. We will bring back our borders. We will bring back our wealth. And we will bring back our dreams.

We will build new roads, and highways, and bridges, and airports, and tunnels, and railways all across our wonderful nation.

We will get our people off of welfare and back to work—rebuilding our country with American hands and American labor.

We will follow two simple rules: Buy American and Hire American.

We will seek friendship and goodwill with the nations of the world—but we do so with the understanding that it is the right of all nations to put their own interests first.

We do not seek to impose our way of life on anyone, but rather to let it shine as an example for everyone to follow.

We will reinforce old alliances and form new ones—and unite the civilized world against Radical Islamic Terrorism, which we will eradicate completely from the face of the Earth.

At the bedrock of our politics will be a total allegiance to the United States of America, and through our loyalty to our country, we will rediscover our loyalty to each other.

When you open your heart to patriotism, there is no room for prejudice.

The Bible tells us, "how good and pleasant it is when God's people live together in unity."

We must speak our minds openly, debate our disagreements honestly, but always pursue solidarity.

When America is united, America is totally unstoppable.

There should be no fear—we are protected, and we will always be protected.

We will be protected by the great men and women of our military and law enforcement and, most importantly, we are protected by God.

Finally, we must think big and dream even bigger.

In America, we understand that a nation is only living as long as it is striving.

We will no longer accept politicians who are all talk and no action—constantly complaining but never doing anything about it.

The time for empty talk is over.

Now arrives the hour of action.

Do not let anyone tell you it cannot be done. No challenge can match the heart and fight and spirit of America.

We will not fail. Our country will thrive and prosper again.

We stand at the birth of a new millennium, ready to unlock the mysteries of space, to free the Earth from the miseries of disease, and to harness the energies, industries and technologies of tomorrow.

A new national pride will stir our souls, lift our sights, and heal our divisions.

It is time to remember that old wisdom our soldiers will never forget: that whether we are black or brown or white, we all bleed the same red blood of patriots, we all enjoy the same glorious freedoms, and we all salute the same great American Flag.

And whether a child is born in the urban sprawl of Detroit or the windswept plains of Nebraska, they look up at the same night sky, they fill their heart with the same dreams, and they are infused with the breath of life by the same almighty Creator.

So to all Americans, in every city near and far, small and large, from mountain to mountain, and from ocean to ocean, hear these words:

You will never be ignored again.

Your voice, your hopes, and your dreams, will define our American destiny. And your courage and goodness and love will forever guide us along the way.

Together, We Will Make America Strong Again.

We Will Make America Wealthy Again.

We Will Make America Proud Again.

We Will Make America Safe Again.

And, Yes, Together, We Will Make America Great Again. Thank you, God Bless You, And God Bless America.

FOR EXERCISE 6

January 13, 2016

Remarks of President Barack Obama—State of the Union Address As Delivered

9:10 p.m. EST

Mr. Speaker, Mr. Vice President, Members of Congress, my fellow Americans:

Tonight marks the eighth year that I've come here to report on the State of the Union. And for this final one, I'm going to try to make it a little shorter. (Applause.) I know some of you are antsy to get back to Iowa. (Laughter.) I've been there. I'll be shaking hands afterwards if you want some tips. (Laughter.)

And I understand that because it's an election season, expectations for what we will achieve this year are low. But, Mr. Speaker, I appreciate the constructive approach that you and the other leaders took at the end of last year to pass a budget and make tax cuts permanent for working families. So I hope we can work together this year on some bipartisan priorities like criminal justice reform—(applause)—and helping people who are battling prescription drug abuse and heroin abuse. (Applause.) So, who knows, we might surprise the cynics again.

But tonight, I want to go easy on the traditional list of proposals for the year ahead. Don't worry, I've got plenty, from helping students learn to write computer code to personalizing medical treatments for patients. And I will keep pushing for progress on the work that I believe still needs to be done. Fixing a broken immigration system. (Applause.) Protecting our kids from gun violence. (Applause.) Equal pay for equal work. (Applause.) Paid leave. (Applause.) Raising the minimum wage. (Applause.) All these things still matter to hardworking families. They're still the right thing to do. And I won't let up until they get done.

But for my final address to this chamber, I don't want to just talk about next year. I want to focus on the next five years, the next 10 years, and beyond. I want to focus on our future.

We live in a time of extraordinary change—change that's reshaping the way we live, the way we work, our planet, our place in the world. It's change that promises amazing medical breakthroughs, but also economic disruptions that strain working families. It promises education for girls in the most remote villages, but also connects terrorists plotting an ocean away. It's change that can broaden opportunity, or widen inequality. And whether we like it or not, the pace of this change will only accelerate.

America has been through big changes before—wars and depression, the influx of new immigrants, workers fighting for a fair deal, movements to expand civil rights. Each time, there have been those who told us to fear the future; who claimed we could slam the brakes on change; who promised to restore past glory if we just got some group or idea that was threatening America under control. And each time, we overcame those fears. We did not, in the words of Lincoln, adhere to the "dogmas of the quiet past." Instead we thought anew, and acted anew. We made change work for us, always extending America's promise outward, to the next frontier, to more people. And because we did—because we saw opportunity where others saw only peril—we emerged stronger and better than before.

What was true then can be true now. Our unique strengths as a nation—our optimism and work ethic, our spirit of discovery, our diversity, our commitment to rule of law—these things give us everything we need to ensure prosperity and security for generations to come.

In fact, it's that spirit that made the progress of these past seven years possible. It's how we recovered from the worst economic crisis in generations. It's how we reformed our health care system, and reinvented our energy sector; how we delivered more care and benefits to our troops and veterans, and how we secured the freedom in every state to marry the person we love.

But such progress is not inevitable. It's the result of choices we make together. And we face such choices right now. Will we respond to the changes of our time with fear, turning inward as a nation, turning against each other as a people? Or will we face the future with confidence in who we are, in what we stand for, in the incredible things that we can do together?

So let's talk about the future, and four big questions that I believe we as a country have to answer—regardless of who the next President is, or who controls the next Congress.

First, how do we give everyone a fair shot at opportunity and security in this new economy? (Applause.)

Second, how do we make technology work for us, and not against us—especially when it comes to solving urgent challenges like climate change? (Applause.)

Third, how do we keep America safe and lead the world without becoming its policeman? (Applause.)

And finally, how can we make our politics reflect what's best in us, and not what's worst?

Let me start with the economy, and a basic fact: The United States of America, right now, has the strongest, most durable economy in the world. (Applause.) We're in the middle of the longest streak of private sector job creation in history. (Applause.) More than 14 million new jobs, the strongest two years of job growth since the '90s, an unemployment rate cut in half. Our auto industry just had its best year ever. (Applause.) That's just part of a manufacturing surge that's created nearly 900,000 new jobs in the past six years. And we've done all this while cutting our deficits by almost three-quarters. (Applause.)

Anyone claiming that America's economy is in decline is peddling fiction. (Applause.) Now, what is true—and the reason that a lot of Americans feel anxious—is that the economy has been changing in profound ways, changes that started long before the Great Recession hit; changes that have not let up.

Today, technology doesn't just replace jobs on the assembly line, but any job where work can be automated. Companies in a global economy can locate anywhere, and they face tougher competition. As a result, workers have less leverage for a raise. Companies have less loyalty to their communities. And more and more wealth and income is concentrated at the very top.

All these trends have squeezed workers, even when they have jobs; even when the economy is growing. It's made it harder for a hardworking family to pull itself out of poverty, harder for young people to start their careers, tougher for workers to retire when they want to. And although none of these trends are unique to America, they do offend our uniquely American belief that everybody who works hard should get a fair shot.

For the past seven years, our goal has been a growing economy that works also better for everybody. We've made progress. But we need to make more. And despite all the political arguments that we've had these past few years, there are actually some areas where Americans broadly agree.

We agree that real opportunity requires every American to get the education and training they need to land a good-paying job. The bipartisan reform of No Child Left Behind was an important start, and together, we've increased early childhood education, lifted high school graduation rates to new highs, boosted graduates in fields like engineering. In the coming years, we should build on that progress, by providing Pre-K for all and—(applause)—offering every student the hands-on computer science and math classes that make them job-ready on day one. We should recruit and support more great teachers for our kids. (Applause.)

And we have to make college affordable for every American. (Applause.) No hardworking student should be stuck in the red. We've already reduced student loan payments to 10 percent of a borrower's income. And that's good. But now, we've actually got to cut the cost of college. (Applause.) Providing two years of community college at no cost for every responsible student is one of the best ways to do that, and I'm going to keep fighting to get that started this year. (Applause.) It's the right thing to do. (Applause.)

But a great education isn't all we need in this new economy. We also need benefits and protections that provide a basic measure of security. It's not too much of a stretch to say that some of the only people in America who are going to work the same job, in the same place, with a health and retirement package for 30 years are sitting in this chamber. (Laughter.) For everyone else, especially folks in their 40s and 50s, saving for retirement or bouncing back from job loss has gotten a lot tougher. Americans understand that at some point in their careers, in this new economy, they may have to retool and they may have to retrain. But they shouldn't lose what they've already worked so hard to build in the process.

That's why Social Security and Medicare are more important than ever. We shouldn't weaken them; we should strengthen them. (Applause.) And for Americans short of retirement, basic benefits should be just as mobile as everything else is today. That, by the way, is what the Affordable Care Act is all about. It's about filling the gaps in employer-based care so that when you lose a job, or you go back to school, or you strike out and launch that new business, you'll still have coverage. Nearly 18 million people have gained coverage so far. (Applause.) And in the process, health care inflation has slowed. And our businesses have created jobs every single month since it became law.

Now, I'm guessing we won't agree on health care anytime soon. (Applause.) A little applause right there. (Laughter.) Just a guess. But there should be other ways parties can work together to improve economic security. Say a hardworking American loses his job—we shouldn't just make sure that he can get unemployment insurance; we should make sure that program encourages him to retrain for a business that's ready to hire him. If that new job doesn't pay as much, there should be a system of wage insurance in place so that he can still pay his bills. And even if he's going from job to job, he should still be able to save for retirement and take his savings with him. That's the way we make the new economy work better for everybody.

I also know Speaker Ryan has talked about his interest in tackling poverty. America is about giving everybody willing to work a chance, a hand up. And I'd welcome a serious discussion about strategies we can all support, like expanding tax cuts for low-income workers who don't have children. (Applause.)

But there are some areas where we just have to be honest—it has been difficult to find agreement over the last seven years. And a lot of them fall under the category of what role the government should play in making sure the system's not rigged in favor of the wealthiest and biggest corporations. (Applause.) And it's an honest disagreement, and the American people have a choice to make.

I believe a thriving private sector is the lifeblood of our economy. I think there are outdated regulations that need to be changed. There is red tape that needs to be cut. (Applause.) There you go! Yes! (Applause.) But after years now of record corporate profits, working families won't get more opportunity or bigger paychecks just by letting big banks or big oil or hedge funds make their own rules at everybody else's expense. (Applause.) Middle-class families are not going to feel more secure because we allowed attacks on collective bargaining to go unanswered. Food Stamp recipients did not cause the financial crisis; recklessness on Wall Street did. (Applause.) Immigrants aren't the principal reason wages haven't gone up; those decisions are made in the boardrooms that all too often put quarterly earnings over long-term returns. It's sure not the average family watching tonight that avoids paying taxes through offshore accounts. (Applause.)

The point is, I believe that in this new economy, workers and start-ups and small businesses need more of a voice, not less. The rules should work for them. (Applause.) And I'm not alone in this. This year I plan to lift up the many businesses who've figured out that doing right by their workers or their customers or their communities ends up being good for their shareholders. (Applause.) And I want to spread those best practices across America. That's part of a brighter future. (Applause.)

In fact, it turns out many of our best corporate citizens are also our most creative. And this brings me to the second big question we as a country have to answer: How do we reignite that spirit of innovation to meet our biggest challenges?

Sixty years ago, when the Russians beat us into space, we didn't deny Sputnik was up there. (Laughter.) We didn't argue about the science, or shrink our research and development budget. We built a space program almost overnight. And 12 years later, we were walking on the moon. (Applause.)

Now, that spirit of discovery is in our DNA. America is Thomas Edison and the Wright Brothers and George Washington Carver. America is Grace Hopper and Katherine Johnson and Sally Ride. America is every immigrant and entrepreneur from Boston to Austin to Silicon Valley, racing to shape a better world. (Applause.) That's who we are.

And over the past seven years, we've nurtured that spirit. We've protected an open Internet, and taken bold new steps to get more students and low-income Americans online. (Applause.) We've launched next-generation manufacturing hubs, and online tools that give an entrepreneur everything he or she needs to start a business in a single day. But we can do so much more.

Last year, Vice President Biden said that with a new moonshot, America can cure cancer. Last month, he worked with this Congress to give scientists at the National Institutes of Health the strongest resources that they've had in over a decade. (Applause.) So tonight, I'm announcing a new national effort to get it done. And because he's gone to the mat for all of us on so many issues over the past 40 years, I'm putting Joe in charge of Mission Control. (Applause.) For the loved ones we've all lost, for the families that we can still save, let's make America the country that cures cancer once and for all. (Applause.)

Medical research is critical. We need the same level of commitment when it comes to developing clean energy sources. (Applause.) Look, if anybody still wants to dispute the science around climate change, have at it. You will be pretty lonely, because you'll be debating our military, most of America's business leaders, the majority of the American people, almost the entire scientific community, and 200 nations around the world who agree it's a problem and intend to solve it. (Applause.)

But even if—even if the planet wasn't at stake, even if 2014 wasn't the warmest year on record—until 2015 turned out to be even hotter—why would we want to pass up the chance for American businesses to produce and sell the energy of the future? (Applause.)

Listen, seven years ago, we made the single biggest investment in clean energy in our history. Here are the results. In fields from Iowa to Texas, wind power is now cheaper than dirtier, conventional power. On rooftops from Arizona to New York, solar is saving Americans tens of millions of dollars a year on their energy bills, and employs more Americans than coal—in jobs that pay better than average. We're taking steps to give homeowners the freedom to generate and store their own energy—something, by the way, that environmentalists and Tea Partiers have teamed up to support. And meanwhile, we've cut our imports of foreign oil by nearly 60 percent, and cut carbon pollution more than any other country on Earth. (Applause.)

Gas under two bucks a gallon ain't bad, either. (Applause.)

Now we've got to accelerate the transition away from old, dirtier energy sources. Rather than subsidize the past, we should invest in the future—especially in communities that rely on fossil fuels. We do them no favor when we don't show them where the trends are going. That's why I'm going to push to change the way we manage our oil and coal resources, so that they better reflect the costs they impose on taxpayers and our planet. And that way, we put money back into those communities, and put tens of thousands of Americans to work building a 21st century transportation system. (Applause.)

Now, none of this is going to happen overnight. And, yes, there are plenty of entrenched interests who want to protect the status quo. But the jobs we'll create, the money we'll save, the planet we'll preserve—that is the kind of future our kids and our grandkids deserve. And it's within our grasp.

Climate change is just one of many issues where our security is linked to the rest of the world. And that's why the third big question that we have to answer together is how to keep America safe and strong without either isolating ourselves or trying to nation-build everywhere there's a problem.

I told you earlier all the talk of America's economic decline is political hot air. Well, so is all the rhetoric you hear about our enemies getting stronger and America getting weaker. Let me tell you something. The United States of America is the most powerful nation on Earth. Period. (Applause.) Period. It's not even close. It's not even close. (Applause.) It's not even close. We spend more on our military than the next eight nations combined. Our troops are the finest fighting force in the history of the world. (Applause.) No nation attacks us directly, or our allies, because they know that's the path to ruin. Surveys show our standing around the world is higher than when I was elected to this office, and when it comes to every important international issue, people of the world do not look to Beijing or Moscow to lead—they call us. (Applause.)

I mean, it's useful to level the set here, because when we don't, we don't make good decisions.

Now, as someone who begins every day with an intelligence briefing, I know this is a dangerous time. But that's not primarily because of some looming superpower out there, and certainly not because of diminished American strength. In today's world, we're threatened less by evil empires and more by failing states.

The Middle East is going through a transformation that will play out for a generation, rooted in conflicts that date back millennia. Economic headwinds are blowing in from a Chinese economy that is in significant transition. Even as their economy severely contracts, Russia is pouring resources in to prop up Ukraine and Syria—client states that they saw slipping away from their orbit. And the international system we built after World War II is now struggling to keep pace with this new reality.

It's up to us, the United States of America, to help remake that system. And to do that well it means that we've got to set priorities.

Priority number one is protecting the American people and going after terrorist networks. (Applause.) Both al Qaeda and now ISIL pose a direct threat to our people, because in today's world, even a handful of terrorists who place no value on human life, including their own, can do a lot of damage. They use the Internet to poison the minds of individuals inside our country. Their actions undermine and destabilize our allies. We have to take them out.

But as we focus on destroying ISIL, over-the-top claims that this is World War III just play into their hands. Masses of fighters on the back of pickup trucks, twisted souls plotting in apartments or garages—they pose an enormous danger to civilians; they have to be stopped. But they do not threaten our national existence. (Applause.) That is the story ISIL wants to tell. That's the kind of propaganda they use to recruit. We don't need to build them up to show that we're serious, and we sure don't need to push away vital allies in this fight by echoing the lie that ISIL is somehow representative of one of the world's largest religions. (Applause.) We just need to call them what they are—killers and fanatics who have to be rooted out, hunted down, and destroyed. (Applause.)

And that's exactly what we're doing. For more than a year, America has led a coalition of more than 60 countries to cut off ISIL's financing, disrupt their plots, stop the flow of terrorist fighters, and stamp out their vicious ideology. With nearly 10,000 air strikes, we're taking out their leadership, their oil, their training camps, their weapons. We're training, arming, and supporting forces who are steadily reclaiming territory in Iraq and Syria.

If this Congress is serious about winning this war, and wants to send a message to our troops and the world, authorize the use of military force against ISIL. Take a vote. (Applause.) Take a vote. But the American people should know that with or without congressional action, ISIL will learn the same lessons as terrorists before them. If you doubt America's commitment—or mine—to see that justice is done, just ask Osama bin Laden. (Applause.) Ask the leader of al Qaeda in Yemen, who was taken out last year, or the perpetrator of the Benghazi attacks, who sits in a prison cell. When you come after Americans, we go after you. (Applause.) And it may take time, but we have long memories, and our reach has no limits. (Applause.)

Our foreign policy has to be focused on the threat from ISIL and al Qaeda, but it can't stop there. For even without ISIL, even without al Qaeda, instability will continue for decades in many parts of the world—in the Middle East, in Afghanistan, parts of Pakistan, in parts of Central America, in Africa, and Asia. Some of these places may become safe havens for new terrorist networks. Others will just fall victim to ethnic conflict, or famine, feeding the next wave of refugees. The world will look to us to help solve these problems, and our answer needs to be more than tough talk or calls to carpet-bomb civilians. That may work as a TV sound bite, but it doesn't pass muster on the world stage.

We also can't try to take over and rebuild every country that falls into crisis, even if it's done with the best of intentions. (Applause.) That's not leadership; that's a recipe for quagmire, spilling American blood and treasure that ultimately will weaken us. It's the lesson of Vietnam; it's the lesson of Iraq—and we should have learned it by now. (Applause.)

Fortunately, there is a smarter approach, a patient and disciplined strategy that uses every element of our national power. It says America will always act, alone if necessary, to protect our people and our allies; but on issues of global concern, we will mobilize the world to work with us, and make sure other countries pull their own weight.

That's our approach to conflicts like Syria, where we're partnering with local forces and leading international efforts to help that broken society pursue a lasting peace.

That's why we built a global coalition, with sanctions and principled diplomacy, to prevent a nuclear-armed Iran. And as we speak, Iran has rolled back its nuclear program, shipped out its uranium stockpile, and the world has avoided another war. (Applause.)

That's how we stopped the spread of Ebola in West Africa. (Applause.) Our military, our doctors, our development workers—they were heroic; they set up the platform that then allowed other countries to join in behind us and stamp out that epidemic. Hundreds of thousands, maybe a couple million lives were saved.

That's how we forged a Trans-Pacific Partnership to open markets, and protect workers and the environment, and advance American leadership in Asia. It cuts 18,000 taxes on products made in America, which will then support more good jobs here in America. With TPP, China does not set the rules in that region; we do. You want to show our strength in this new century? Approve this agreement. Give us the tools to enforce it. It's the right thing to do. (Applause.)

Let me give you another example. Fifty years of isolating Cuba had failed to promote democracy, and set us back in Latin America. That's why we restored diplomatic relations—(applause)—opened the door to travel and commerce, positioned ourselves to improve the lives of the Cuban people. (Applause.) So if you want to consolidate our leadership and credibility in the hemisphere, recognize that the Cold War is over—lift the embargo. (Applause.)

The point is American leadership in the 21st century is not a choice between ignoring the rest of the world—except when we kill terrorists—or occupying and rebuilding whatever society is unraveling. Leadership means a wise application of military power, and rallying the world behind causes that are right. It means seeing our foreign assistance as a part of our national security, not something separate, not charity.

When we lead nearly 200 nations to the most ambitious agreement in history to fight climate change, yes, that helps vulnerable countries, but it also protects our kids. When we help Ukraine defend its democracy, or Colombia resolve a decades-long war, that strengthens the international order we depend on. When we help African countries feed their people and care for the sick—(applause)—it's the right thing to do, and it prevents the next pandemic from reaching our shores. Right now, we're on track to end the scourge of HIV/AIDS. That's within our grasp. (Applause.) And we have the chance to accomplish the same thing with malaria—something I'll be pushing this Congress to fund this year. (Applause.)

That's American strength. That's American leadership. And that kind of leadership depends on the power of our example. That's why I will keep working to shut down the prison at Guantanamo. (Applause.) It is expensive, it is unnecessary, and it only serves as a recruitment brochure for our enemies. (Applause.) There's a better way. (Applause.)

And that's why we need to reject any politics—any politics—that targets people because of race or religion. (Applause.) Let me just say this. This is not a matter of political correctness. This is a matter of understanding just what it is that makes us strong. The world respects us not just for our arsenal; it respects us for our diversity, and our openness, and the way we respect every faith.

His Holiness, Pope Francis, told this body from the very spot that I'm standing on tonight that "to imitate the hatred and violence of tyrants and murderers is the best way to take their place." When politicians insult Muslims, whether abroad or our fellow citizens, when a mosque is vandalized, or a kid is called names, that doesn't make us safer. That's not telling it like it is. It's just wrong. (Applause.) It diminishes us in the eyes of the world. It makes it harder to achieve our goals. It betrays who we are as a country. (Applause.)

"We the People." Our Constitution begins with those three simple words, words we've come to recognize mean all the people, not just some; words that insist we rise and fall together, and that's how we might perfect our Union. And that brings me to the fourth, and maybe the most important thing that I want to say tonight.

The future we want—all of us want—opportunity and security for our families, a rising standard of living, a sustainable, peaceful planet for our kids—all that is within our reach. But it will only happen if we work together. It will only happen if we can have rational, constructive debates. It will only happen if we fix our politics.

A better politics doesn't mean we have to agree on everything. This is a big country—different regions, different attitudes, different interests. That's one of our strengths, too. Our Founders distributed power between states and branches of government, and expected us to argue, just as they did, fiercely, over the size and shape of government, over commerce and foreign relations, over the meaning of liberty and the imperatives of security.

But democracy does require basic bonds of trust between its citizens. It doesn't work if we think the people who disagree with us are all motivated by malice. It doesn't work if we think that our political opponents are unpatriotic or trying to weaken America. Democracy grinds to a halt without a willingness to compromise, or when even basic facts are contested, or when we listen only to those who agree with us. Our public life withers when only the most extreme voices get all the attention. And most of all, democracy breaks down when the average person feels their voice doesn't matter; that the system is rigged in favor of the rich or the powerful or some special interest.

Too many Americans feel that way right now. It's one of the few regrets of my presidency—that the rancor and suspicion between the parties has gotten worse instead of better. I have no doubt a president with the gifts of Lincoln or Roosevelt might have better bridged the divide, and I guarantee I'll keep trying to be better so long as I hold this office.

But, my fellow Americans, this cannot be my task—or any President's—alone. There are a whole lot of folks in this chamber, good people who would like to see more cooperation, would like to see a more elevated debate in Washington, but feel trapped by the imperatives of getting elected, by the noise coming out of your base. I know; you've told me. It's the worst-kept secret in Washington. And a lot of you aren't enjoying being trapped in that kind of rancor.

But that means if we want a better politics—and I'm addressing the American people now—if we want a better politics, it's not enough just to change a congressman or change a senator or even change a President. We have to change the system to reflect our better selves. I think we've got to end the practice of drawing our congressional districts so that politicians can pick their voters, and not the other way around. (Applause.) Let a bipartisan group do it. (Applause.)

We have to reduce the influence of money in our politics, so that a handful of families or hidden interests can't bankroll our elections. (Applause.) And if our existing approach to campaign finance reform can't pass muster in the courts, we need to work together to find a real solution—because it's a problem. And most of you don't like raising money. I know; I've done it. (Applause.) We've got to make it easier to vote, not harder. (Applause.) We need to modernize it for the way we live now. (Applause.) This is America: We want to make it easier for people to participate. And over the course of this year, I intend to travel the country to push for reforms that do just that.

But I can't do these things on my own. (Applause.) Changes in our political process—in not just who gets elected, but how they get elected—that will only happen when the American people demand it. It depends on you. That's what's meant by a government of, by, and for the people.

What I'm suggesting is hard. It's a lot easier to be cynical; to accept that change is not possible, and politics is hopeless, and the problem is all the folks who are elected don't care, and to believe that our voices and actions don't matter. But if we give up now, then we forsake a better future. Those with money and power will gain greater control over the decisions that could send a young soldier to war, or allow another economic disaster, or roll back the equal rights and voting rights that generations of Americans have fought, even died, to secure. And then, as frustration grows, there will be voices urging us to fall back into our respective tribes, to scapegoat fellow citizens who don't look like us, or pray like us, or vote like we do, or share the same background.

We can't afford to go down that path. It won't deliver the economy we want. It will not produce the security we want. But most of all, it contradicts everything that makes us the envy of the world.

So, my fellow Americans, whatever you may believe, whether you prefer one party or no party, whether you supported my agenda or fought as hard as you could against it—our collective futures depends on your willingness to uphold your duties as a citizen. To vote. To speak out. To stand up for others, especially the weak, especially the vulnerable, knowing that each of us is only here because somebody, somewhere, stood up for us. (Applause.) We need every American to stay active in our public life—and not just during election time—so that our public life reflects the goodness and the decency that I see in the American people every single day.

It is not easy. Our brand of democracy is hard. But I can promise that a little over a year from now, when I no longer hold this office, I will be right there with you as a citizen, inspired by those voices of fairness and vision, of grit and good humor and kindness that helped

America travel so far. Voices that help us see ourselves not, first and foremost, as black or white, or Asian or Latino, not as gay or straight, immigrant or native born, not as Democrat or Republican, but as Americans first, bound by a common creed. Voices Dr. King believed would have the final word—voices of unarmed truth and unconditional love.

And they're out there, those voices. They don't get a lot of attention; they don't seek a lot of fanfare; but they're busy doing the work this country needs doing. I see them everywhere I travel in this incredible country of ours. I see you, the American people. And in your daily acts of citizenship, I see our future unfolding.

I see it in the worker on the assembly line who clocked extra shifts to keep his company open, and the boss who pays him higher wages instead of laying him off.

I see it in the Dreamer who stays up late to finish her science project, and the teacher who comes in early because he knows she might someday cure a disease.

I see it in the American who served his time, and made mistakes as a child but now is dreaming of starting over—and I see it in the business owner who gives him that second chance. The protester determined to prove that justice matters—and the young cop walking the beat, treating everybody with respect, doing the brave, quiet work of keeping us safe. (Applause.)

I see it in the soldier who gives almost everything to save his brothers, the nurse who tends to him till he can run a marathon, the community that lines up to cheer him on.

It's the son who finds the courage to come out as who he is, and the father whose love for that son overrides everything he's been taught. (Applause.)

I see it in the elderly woman who will wait in line to cast her vote as long as she has to; the new citizen who casts his vote for the first time; the volunteers at the polls who believe every vote should count—because each of them in different ways know how much that precious right is worth.

That's the America I know. That's the country we love. Clear-eyed. Big-hearted. Undaunted by challenge. Optimistic that unarmed truth and unconditional love will have the final word. (Applause.) That's what makes me so hopeful about our future. I believe in change because I believe in you, the American people.

And that's why I stand here confident as I have ever been that the State of our Union is strong. (Applause.)

Thank you, God bless you. God bless the United States of America.

###

Gov. Nikki Haley's response to the State of the Union

South Carolina Gov. Nikki Haley provided the Republican response to President Barack Obama's State of the Union address (included above). The speech occurred on the same day as the SOTU, shortly after the president finished. Below is a transcript of that speech.

I'm Nikki Haley, Governor of the great state of South Carolina.

I'm speaking tonight from Columbia, our state's capital city. Much like America as a whole, ours is a state with a rich and complicated history, one that proves the idea that each day can be better than the last.

In just a minute, I'm going to talk about a vision of a brighter American future. But first I want to say a few words about President Obama, who just gave his final State of the Union address.

Barack Obama's election as president seven years ago broke historic barriers and inspired millions of Americans. As he did when he first ran for office, tonight President Obama spoke eloquently about grand things. He is at his best when he does that.

Unfortunately, the President's record has often fallen far short of his soaring words.

As he enters his final year in office, many Americans are still feeling the squeeze of an economy too weak to raise income levels. We're feeling a crushing national debt, a health care plan that has made insurance less affordable and doctors less available, and chaotic unrest in many of our cities.

Even worse, we are facing the most dangerous terrorist threat our nation has seen since September 11th, and this president appears either unwilling or unable to deal with it.

Soon, the Obama presidency will end, and America will have the chance to turn in a new direction. That direction is what I want to talk about tonight.

At the outset, I'll say this: you've paid attention to what has been happening in Washington, and you're not naive.

Neither am I. I see what you see. And many of your frustrations are my frustrations.

A frustration with a government that has grown day after day, year after year, yet doesn't serve us any better. A frustration with the same, endless conversations we hear over and over again. A frustration with promises made and never kept.

We need to be honest with each other, and with ourselves: while Democrats in Washington bear much responsibility for the problems facing America today, they do not bear it alone. There is more than enough blame to go around.

We as Republicans need to own that truth. We need to recognize our contributions to the erosion of the public trust in America's leadership. We need to accept that we've played a role in how and why our government is broken.

And then we need to fix it.

The foundation that has made America that last, best hope on earth hasn't gone anywhere. It still exists. It is up to us to return to it.

For me, that starts right where it always has: I am the proud daughter of Indian immigrants who reminded my brothers, my sister and me every day how blessed we were to live in this country.

Growing up in the rural south, my family didn't look like our neighbors, and we didn't have much. There were times that were tough, but we had each other, and we had the opportunity to do anything, to be anything, as long as we were willing to work for it.

My story is really not much different from millions of other Americans. Immigrants have been coming to our shores for generations to live the dream that is America. They wanted better for their children than for themselves. That remains the dream of all of us, and in this country we have seen time and again that that dream is achievable.

Today, we live in a time of threats like few others in recent memory. During anxious times, it can be tempting to follow the siren call of the angriest voices. We must resist that temptation.

No one who is willing to work hard, abide by our laws, and love our traditions should ever feel unwelcome in this country.

At the same time, that does not mean we just flat out open our borders. We can't do that. We cannot continue to allow immigrants to come here illegally. And in this age of terrorism, we must not let in refugees whose intentions cannot be determined.

We must fix our broken immigration system. That means stopping illegal immigration. And it means welcoming properly vetted legal immigrants, regardless of their race or religion. Just like we have for centuries.

I have no doubt that if we act with proper focus, we can protect our borders, our sovereignty and our citizens, all while remaining true to America's noblest legacies.

This past summer, South Carolina was dealt a tragic blow. On an otherwise ordinary Wednesday evening in June, at the historic Mother Emanuel church in Charleston, twelve faithful men and women, young and old, went to Bible study.

That night, someone new joined them. He didn't look like them, didn't act like them, didn't sound like them. They didn't throw him out. They didn't call the police. Instead, they pulled up a chair and prayed with him. For an hour.

We lost nine incredible souls that night.

What happened after the tragedy is worth pausing to think about.

Our state was struck with shock, pain, and fear. But our people would not allow hate to win. We didn't have violence, we had vigils. We didn't have riots, we had hugs.

We didn't turn against each other's race or religion. We turned toward God, and to the values that have long made our country the freest and greatest in the world.

We removed a symbol that was being used to divide us, and we found a strength that united us against a domestic terrorist and the hate that filled him.

There's an important lesson in this. In many parts of society today, whether in popular culture, academia, the media, or politics, there's a tendency to falsely equate noise with results.

Some people think that you have to be the loudest voice in the room to make a difference. That is just not true. Often, the best thing we can do is turn down the volume. When the sound is quieter, you can actually hear what someone else is saying. And that can make a world of difference.

Of course that doesn't mean we won't have strong disagreements. We will. And as we usher in this new era, Republicans will stand up for our beliefs.

If we held the White House, taxes would be lower for working families, and we'd put the brakes on runaway spending and debt.

We would encourage American innovation and success instead of demonizing them, so our economy would truly soar and good jobs would be available across our country.

We would reform education so it worked best for students, parents, and teachers, not Washington bureaucrats and union bosses.

We would end a disastrous health care program, and replace it with reforms that lowered costs and actually let you keep your doctor.

We would respect differences in modern families, but we would also insist on respect for religious liberty as a cornerstone of our democracy.

We would recognize the importance of the separation of powers and honor the Constitution in its entirety. And yes, that includes the Second and Tenth Amendments.

We would make international agreements that were celebrated in Israel and protested in Iran, not the other way around.

And rather than just thanking our brave men and women in uniform, we would actually strengthen our military, so both our friends and our enemies would know that America seeks peace, but when we fight wars we win them.

We have big decisions to make. Our country is being tested.

But we've been tested in the past, and our people have always risen to the challenge. We have all the guidance we need to be safe and successful.

Our forefathers paved the way for us.

Let's take their values, and their strengths, and rededicate ourselves to doing whatever it takes to keep America the greatest country in the history of man. And woman.

Thank you, good night, and God bless.

EXPANDED NEWS WRITING

REVIEW

1. What are the three things your book lists as potential bridge elements for your story? When should you use each of the bridge types?

2. What are the two ways the book recommends to close a story? When should you use each closing type?

3. How does the "kabob" approach to narrative writing work?

4. What is a nut graph, and what purpose does it serve?

5. Define and differentiate between linear and nonlinear storytelling. Outline the benefits and drawbacks of each.

WRITING EXERCISES

1. Select a long-form narrative story from a website or a magazine and analyze it.

    - Does it follow a "kabob" approach? Does it contain a narrative thread? Does it have a nut graph?

    - If it contains each element, how strong or weak is that element? How could the reporter have done better?

    - If you note that an element is missing, how did the writer still effectively tell the story? Was the story harmed by the missing element?

2. Find a story with descriptive elements to it. The descriptions could be of an area, a process, a person or anything else.

    - Based on the descriptions offered to you, can you see what the author is describing in your mind's eye?

    - What did the writer do to paint a "word picture" that was effective in helping you see this item?

    - If you feel that something was lacking, what was it, and what could the writer have done better?

3. Pick a topic of interest to you that could make for an interesting and compelling story for an audience of your choosing (e.g., fans of a sports team, students at your college or university). Then sketch out a story web that touches on various aspects of that topic. The core should be the central junction point of the main ideas, but secondary areas can serve as hubs for additional topics as well. Then, write up a short essay that explains what would go into each of these areas, what tools would do the best job for each of these topics and how you think this approach would best serve your audience.

4. Follow Tony Rehagen's advice: Read a narrative, long-form story and then read through the comments after it.

    - Which comments make sense, and which ones, as Rehagen said, are "garbage" posts?

    - How much do you agree with the commenters, and how much do you disagree?

- How could the writer have improved the story to meet the demands of the commenters?
- What would have made the story better in your mind?

5. Consider the following chunks of text that could be nut graphs for "bigger topic" stories. For each of these chunks, identify the types of people who could serve as a good narrative thread for your story. For example, a bigger story might examine cuts to specific state scholarships for nontraditional students and federal cuts for higher education. For a narrative thread, you might consider finding a returning student who is on a state scholarship and is using the GI Bill to pay for part of her education.

   a. The city council is considering a proposal to ban the ownership of ferrets after several of the animals died because of poor treatment at one of the city's pet shops. If passed, the law would also make it illegal to buy, sell or own other animals in the weasel family as pets.

   b. Your campus is revising its parking regulations and permit procedure to discourage students from driving to campus. It has shortened meter times so that students cannot park in metered spaces for a full class period without "plugging the meter" a second time. It has placed residency restrictions on passes that prohibit students who live within a three-block radius of campus from purchasing a parking pass. It has cut in half the number of parking permits that will be issued to students who do not commute.

   c. In the wake of several outbreaks of food-borne illness, the city health department has cracked down on food services in your area. Any person serving food, including waitresses and food-truck service workers, must pass a new health department course before being allowed to work. Food sold as part of charity fundraisers, such as church festivals and student baked-good fundraisers, is banned from public sale. Any contest involving food, such as a pie-eating contest or a chili cook-off, must be preapproved by a city health inspector, at a cost of $100 per inspection.

6. **WORD-PICTURE EXERCISE**

   Pick three different products that supposedly have the same base scent. For example, you could pick a citrus candy, a piece of citrus fruit and a citrus-based cleaner. Smell each one of them independent of the others, and then make a list of what words come to mind. Look for descriptors that would clearly tie them together, such as "tart" or "sharp," as well as descriptors that distinguish them from one another, such as "fresh" or "artificial." Come up with a list of words for these scents that you think would help you paint a good word picture based on smell.

SOCIAL MEDIA

REVIEW

1. What are some of the hints online marketing guru John Rampton offers for building a social media audience? Of the items listed in the chapter, which one do you think is most important? Why?

2. What are the suggestions the chapter offers you for how to use Twitter as a reporter? Which suggestion mirrors an approach you are already taking on social media? Which suggestion gave you a new idea to try?

3. What is a blog? How is it similar to and different from traditional mass media such as newspapers or magazines?

4. What are the three suggestions your book offers you for how best to use social media for your audience? Which of the three do you think is most important? Why?

WRITING EXERCISES

1. Analyze two social media platforms you actively use to receive content.

   • What people (or kinds of people) do you follow on each platform? What do they provide to you as a receiver of information?

   • To what degree do they meet some of the standards John Rampton outlined for audience building? What made you confer authority and trust upon the people you follow?

   • How much overlap is there between the two platforms you are examining in terms of content, people you follow and interest areas? Why do you think this is the case?

2. Analyze a social media platform you actively use to share information.

   • How many people follow you, and what do you know about those people?

   • How often do you think about your audience before you post content? When you look at your content, to what degree is it accessible to your readers or viewers in terms of journalistic basics (spelling, grammar and style)?

   • Given what you read in the chapter, would you change your approach to sharing content on this platform? Why or why not?

3. Research a case of a false story going viral through social media. Include some background on the story itself, the person who started the false story and how far the story got before people realized it was false.

   • What were some of the bigger news organizations or media outlets that were duped by this story?

   • What could have been done to prevent the story from spiraling beyond a few people or groups?

4. The concept of social media "bubbles" has become prominent as people insulate themselves from ideas they dislike. This has led to serious disconnects between groups of people regarding things like politics, international affairs and societal norms.

- What are the benefits and drawbacks of social media with regard to the "bubble" phenomenon? How do you keep yourself informed on topics of broader interest without getting trapped in an echo chamber of only supportive ideas?

- Do you have trouble interacting with people who are too deeply trapped within their own "bubbles" of information? How do you think this problem can be solved?

5. Review a series of blogs in an area of interest to you.

   - Assess them with regard to how well they focus on audience interests, establish a tone, provide timely information and offer quick reads.

   - Then, see if you can either join the blog's staff of writers for a short period of time or start your own blog in that area. Before you begin writing, however, make sure you can establish a niche you feel is underserved in this area of coverage.

   - Also, sketch out a few topics you plan to cover in your first few posts. Augment your posts with links to other sites that support your thoughts and ideas.

   - Monitor your traffic and the comments on your site for any readership. Use your other social media outlets to garner readership and to connect with interested parties.

6. **TWITTER PRACTICE**

   Below are several chunks of information that could be used as part of a story on a news website. Review the information and create a tweet for each chunk. Keep your tweets to a maximum of 250 characters, as you want to save space for retweets and a link to the story. Use the suggestions in the chapter regarding structure, style and emphasis as you write your tweets.

   a. The head of Computerville Corp. visited campus today as part of the school's "Understanding the Future" speaker series. John Wahl, founder, president and CEO of the organization, spoke at length about how computers have dominated technological advances over the past 30 years. His company, for example, grew from five employees working out of his mother's basement to one of the top three software developers in the world in just 20 years. During his speech, he outlined how his company came to be, how it grew so quickly and what it is doing now. He explained that by the end of this year, his company would be the first to roll out computer software that allows planes to fly without pilots and boats to traverse the ocean without a crew.

b. The Okra City Police Department responded to a call of an accident at the intersection of Main Street and Johnson Avenue around 9:14 a.m. Police found that a 2017 Cadillac Escalade had failed to stop at a four-way stop and slammed into the side of a 2003 Chevy passenger van carrying a group of Amiright Elementary School students heading to the zoo for a field trip. Of the 14 students on board, six were seriously injured and two others died at the scene. The driver of the Cadillac was Bert Bingly, Okra's mayor. He sustained minor injuries and was arrested on suspicion of drinking and driving as well as vehicular homicide.

c. The Allenton Asps baseball team played its final game of the season Sunday. After falling behind by 12 runs in the second inning to the visiting Beaverton Bees, the manager removed all of his starting players and used the second-string team to finish the game. In the next seven innings, the Asps scored 13 runs while the pitching shut out the Bees. The Asps completed the greatest comeback in the history of the Appalachian League, winning 13-12.

7. **BROADER SOCIAL MEDIA WRITING EXERCISE**

Pick one story from each of the sports, news and features sections of a website, and construct a tweet, a Facebook post and a blog entry that would serve to enhance or promote the content from each piece you selected. Remember, each platform has specific benefits and drawbacks, so pay attention to them as you develop your approach. You want these three pieces to work collaboratively as opposed to merely repeating the material on all three platforms.

INTERVIEWING

REVIEW

1. What are the three crucial questions your book lists with regard to critically thinking about an interview's purpose? How does each of them affect your approach to an interview?

2. What are the pros and cons of an email interview? When should you use them, and when should you avoid them?

3. What is a loaded question, and why is it bad?

4. When you contact someone to set up an interview, what should you tell this person about you and your needs relating to that interview?

5. What is the primary difference between an open-ended question and a closed-ended question? When is it appropriate to use each of them?

6. According to your book, about how many prepared questions should you have for a standard news interview?

WRITING EXERCISES

1. Review the five interview types outlined in the book and select two of them.

    - Compare and contrast these interviews, including such things as the benefits and drawbacks of each, the ease of conducting them and the amount of time each is likely to take.

    - Which type of interview do you think is the easiest to conduct? The hardest? Why?

2. Reread the section in the book regarding the obituaries written in the wake of the shooting at Virginia Tech. Kelly Furnas noted that his students were terrified of interviewing family and friends of the deceased, but he said that the interviews were important. He noted that reporters couldn't assume that people would be unwilling to talk and that reporters shouldn't take that chance away from them because of the reporters' own fear. How likely is it that you think you would be able to interview someone shortly after a family member or friend died? What would make you concerned, and how would you deal with it? Do you agree or disagree with Furnas' statement about needing to offer people the opportunity to speak in the wake of an incident like the shooting? Why?

3. Below is a list of poorly worded questions. Rewrite each to fix the problems associated with it (or come up with a better overall question), and then explain why your version of the question is better than the initial question.

    a. "Coach, how many more bad decisions does Quarterback Brett Belter have to make until you bench him?"

b. "Senator, talk about the rationale behind your bill that would ban the use of nut-based products on airplanes after one of your grandchildren went into anaphylactic shock during a flight."

c. "Mr. Jones, I know your wife just died in a car accident. How do you feel about that?"

d. "President Trump, did you ever think you would become president of the United States?"

e. "After three losses in a row, Coach, don't you think the fans have a right to demand that you be fired?"

f. "When you first met your husband, were you alone at the diner, or were you just by yourself?"

g. "Mr. Mayor, you had concerns about the voting process, which some people said was rigged, but do you feel that's not true now only because you won?"

h. "When were you born on your birthday?"

i. "How many of your comeback wins came when the other team was ahead?"

j. "I know your company was purchased recently by a group out of Japan, China or Canada, so which one was it?"

4. Watch a news interview that a broadcast journalist conducted live on air. It could be during a Sunday morning talk show or a longer clip on YouTube. Analyze the purpose of the interview and the value of the individual who is being interviewed in relation to the topic.

a. Do you think the interview worked well overall? Why or why not?

b. How did the interviewer use questions and statements to gather information?

c. Select one or two questions you think were particularly good, and explain why you thought they worked.

d. Pick one or two questions you think were particularly problematic, and explain how you would have reworked the questions to improve them.

5. Below are several scenarios in which a source is asking you to go "off the record." For each case, state if you would or would not go off the record, and explain the reasoning behind your choice.

a. A worker in the governor's office says she has information for you about a recent land purchase the state made. She is concerned that this purchase might not be legal or ethical, as it appears to benefit certain people "close to the governor." She doesn't want to have her name appear with this story, for fear of being fired, but she won't give you any more information unless you go off the record.

b. Two weeks before an election, you receive a call from a staff member of a senator's campaign. The senator is locked in a tight race with his opponent, and the staff member says she has some "juicy" information about the senator's opponent that she is willing to share only with you. The staff member says she will share the information with you only if it will not be attributed in any way to her or the campaign.

c. A recent spate of graffiti has hit your town, with these spray-paint artists covering businesses, train cars and even public property. A friend of yours says he can get you an interview with one of the most prominent members of this underground group. The graffiti artist, however, has requested anonymity because he doesn't want to get caught.

d. You are sent to cover a local craft fair, and you want to tell the story of local crafters. A man who does chainsaw sculptures of bears has drawn a lot of attention at the fair and seems to be making the most sales. You ask the man for an interview, and he immediately asks, "Is this going to be off the record? Otherwise, I'm not talking to you."

6. **INTERVIEWING EXERCISE**

Select a person of interest to you and work your way through the interview process listed in the chapter with him or her.

a. Start by asking for an interview via email or telephone. Include your interview's purpose, your deadline and how much time you will need for the interview.

b. Find a place to interview the person face to face.

c. Prepare for the interview by researching the person and crafting about four or five good questions based on your research.

d. Conduct the interview, and take good notes. If possible, record the interview as well so you can compare your notes with what the person actually said.

e. After the interview, write an inverted-pyramid piece on this interview. Use a solid lead to capture the theme of the interview, and build the remainder of the piece in paraphrase-quote pairings. Make sure to properly attribute your quotes and paraphrases. This piece should be 1.5 to 2 pages long.

7. **SECOND-DAY WRITING EXERCISE**

Pick a topic of interest and conduct several short "person on the street" interviews with the purpose of getting one or two good quotes from each subject. Keep in mind, the overall value of the topic to the interview subjects and the knowledge these people have of the subject will influence the quality of the interviews. With that in mind, you want to pick topics that will likely matter to the interview subjects and topics that have been relevant to them as well. For example, if you live in a small town that has a prominent high school basketball team headed for the state finals, you will likely find a lot of people with opinions on the topic. However, if you are asking people in that same town about the overall impact Russian aggression is having in Crimea, you might get less of a response. Once you complete your interviews, write a solid second-day story. Use the appropriate style of lead, in which you focus on the theme of the reaction and build an expanded inverted-pyramid story from your interview material. Follow the paraphrase-quote pattern described earlier.

BASIC REPORTING:
NEWS THAT FINDS YOU

REVIEW

1. In preparing for a basic reporting assignment, what are some sources you should use to research the event?

2. Your book mentions that you should "be sure you are sure" when it comes to basic facts. What are some of the things the chapter says you should do to keep inaccuracies out of your copy?

3. What are the three types of nonsporting events your book notes that you will likely cover as a beginning reporter? How are they similar? How are they different?

4. What are the key items you should include in a story about a sporting event?

5. What are the two pieces of advice your book offers when it comes to covering a crime or disaster?

6. What are the key items you should include in a crime or disaster story?

WRITING EXERCISES

1. Review the section of this chapter pertaining to news conferences. Based on the problems noted with this form of event, do you think news conferences are worth covering? What are some ways to improve your overall news-conference coverage that would help you sidestep these problems?

2. Read the information on the FAA press statement on the Galaxy Note7 issue (see page 47). Make a list of ways in which you could localize this story, including potential sources.

3. **SPEECH STORY PRACTICE**

   On page 48 there is a transcript of a speech delivered by Deputy Attorney General Rod Rosenstein at the U.S. Marshals Service Inaugural Memorial Service. Read the material carefully and then construct a simple one-source speech story, using an inverted-pyramid format, a solid lead and good paraphrase-quote pairings.

4. **CRIME-WRITING PRACTICE**

   Use the information on page 50 on a local crime to create a simple disaster story. Incorporate two human sources and make sure to attribute your information properly, especially if you are discussing key aspects of the crime.

5. **LIVE SPEECH STORY EXERCISE**

   Locate a public speech of interest to you and research the event.
   - Find out as much as you can about the speaker, the topic and the group sponsoring the event.

- Make contact with the group hosting the speaker and interview someone there about the value of this speaker.
- Then, attend the speech and cover the event with the intention of writing a two-source speech story.

6. **LIVE MEETING STORY EXERCISE**

Locate and cover a public meeting near you.

- Get a copy of an agenda in advance of the event.
- Examine the agenda for key items you think would be valuable and interesting to readers in your area.
- Research those topics through previous news articles, governmental websites and other sources to better understand the items you selected.
- Attend the meeting with the purpose of writing an inverted-pyramid story on the outcome of the event. The story should contain quotes from no fewer than two sources and should incorporate at least three paragraphs of background from the information you gathered in advance of the event.

7. **LIVE LOCALIZATION STORY EXERCISE**

Select a national story that you think has a local impact. (For example, when Canada reworked its tariffs on dairy products to limit U.S. imports, news outlets in Wisconsin interviewed local farmers about the changes and how the local farm economy would be affected.)

- Research your area for sources you think could provide a local angle for you, and then interview at least three of those people.
- Write a localization story that uses a localization lead and solid background from the national story and provides good insight from your local sources. You should include at least two human sources as well as at least two paragraphs of background from the material you gathered.

8. **LIVE SPORTS STORY EXERCISE**

Attend a local sporting event at a high school or college and write a game story on it.

- Be sure to keep track of the key statistics and make special note of the star players throughout the game.

- At the end of the game, conduct at least two interviews with players and/or coaches based on the outcome of the game and your observations throughout it.
- Then, write a gamer that incorporates the key elements required for this type of story that were listed in the chapter. Incorporate quotes from at least two human sources. The story should be between 2 and 2.5 pages, typed, double-spaced.

FOR EXERCISE 2

Press Release—FAA Statement

For Immediate Release

January 10, 2017

The FAA said today that U.S. airlines would no longer be required to make a pre-boarding notification to passengers that the Samsung Galaxy Note7 phone is prohibited from transport on aircraft. The devices are still prohibited on both passenger and air cargo aircraft, but the DOT has lifted the requirement that the airlines make the specific pre-boarding notification.

The Department of Transportation removed the requirement for air carriers to specifically notify passengers about the Note7 phone immediately prior to boarding due to the high degree of public awareness of the ban since issuance of the emergency restriction/prohibition order, as well as the extensive efforts by Samsung and U.S. wireless providers to make all Note7 users aware the phone is recalled and banned from transport on U.S. aircraft. The awareness of the ban is evidenced by the significant rate of recall returns.

The Department of Transportation issued an emergency restriction/prohibition order effective on October 14, 2016, designating the Samsung Galaxy Note7 phone as forbidden on aircraft. The order had several requirements:

- It prohibited the shipment of Note7 as air cargo, and prohibited airline passengers from carrying the Note7 on their person, in carry-on baggage, or in checked baggage.

- It also required that airlines notify passengers immediately before boarding that the Note7 was forbidden.

Samsung said that it has successfully recalled more than 96% of all Note7 devices in the U.S. since this order went into effect, and U.S. wireless providers have pushed out firmware created by Samsung that prevents batteries on the remaining devices from charging.

The Samsung Galaxy Note7 will still be banned on passenger aircraft as well as air cargo aircraft. Only the specific pre-boarding notifications will cease to be mandatory.

###

FOR EXERCISE 3

Arlington, VA

Friday, May 12, 2017

Thank you, Acting Director [Dave] Harlow, for that introduction. And thank you for your more than 30 years of service to the Marshals Service.

We are gathered—during this Police Week—to pay special tribute to the memory of Deputy Commander Patrick Carothers.

I especially want to thank Terry, Jessica, Conner and the entire Carothers family. You helped Patrick become the man that he was. And the strength that you have shown at this difficult time is nothing short of amazing.

Today, we recall his 20 years of service as a Deputy U.S. Marshal and for his service as Deputy Commander of the Southeast Regional Fugitive Task Force.

As we do that, we also remember what it means to be a U.S. Marshal.

Marshals catch fugitives on the run. They keep our courthouses, our judges and our witnesses safe.

It was the Marshals who brought peace and order to the Wild West. It was the Marshals who stood guard during the Civil Rights Movement, protecting innocent people.

That tradition of keeping our communities safe has continued unbroken since 1789. Just in the last decade, U.S. Marshals have arrested more than one million violent fugitives. They have recovered hundreds of missing children. They have safely transported more than 2.5 million detainees and inmates, and protected our communities by completing more than 300,000 compliance checks on registered sex offenders.

They do these things at great risk—at the risk even of their lives. And they know that. They and their families know that only too well.

It takes courage to wear a badge for even one day. It takes a lot more courage to wear it for 20 years, like Patrick Carothers did.

He lost his life while trying to arrest a suspect wanted on charges of attempted murder—attempted murder of police officers.

When I heard about his loss, I was reminded of the man who is synonymous with the Marshals service: Robert Forsyth.

Robert Forsyth was, of course, Patrick's predecessor. He was the very first U.S. Marshal for Georgia, appointed by President George Washington.

He was also the first U.S. Marshal killed in the line of duty, and the namesake of the Marshals Service's award for valor.

He died while serving papers to two men in Augusta. One of the men saw him coming, and in a cowardly act, fired his weapon through the door, killing Forsyth instantly.

More than 400 Marshals and Deputy Marshals have made that same sacrifice since that day. Each of them was an American hero.

Deputy Commander Carothers was an American hero, too.

He died during an important mission—bringing to justice a dangerous and violent criminal.

After so many years in law enforcement, he could have retired or gotten a desk job. But that just wasn't for him.

That day—and so many other days—Deputy Commander Carothers led from the front. He was the first officer through the door in pursuing the suspect.

He left behind him what he was most proud of: his wife of 30 years, Terry and their five children.

I think it's clear that he handed down to his children his commitment to serving this country. All three of Patrick and Terry's grown sons—Lieutenant Michael Carothers, Ensign Matthew Carothers and Midshipman Paul Carothers—are serving our country in the Navy. In fact, they couldn't be here today because they are currently serving. But they are certainly with us in spirit.

The tragedy happened on November 18th, just before Thanksgiving, when we as Americans set aside time to gather with family and give thanks for our blessings.

That time of year will never be the same for this family. They will never stop missing him. But neither will they ever forget his heroic example.

Nor will the more than 2,000 people who came to his funeral. Nor will we.

We won't forget what he did, and we won't forget who he was.

If you talk to his fellow Marshals and Deputy Marshals who knew him, they'll tell you that Patrick was always quick with a smile, and that, if you offered him a handshake, he might just give you a hug instead.

They'll also tell you just how proud he was to be a member of America's oldest and most versatile federal law enforcement agency.

And as proud as he was to be a U.S. Marshal, the Marshals Service is even more proud of him—to have had someone like him wear the badge.

Today we unveil his name on the Marshals Service Wall of Honor. Whenever people come to headquarters, they will see his name. And when they see his name, they will think about his example, what he did for us. I hope that will inspire us to imitate his bravery, his dedication and his love of country. Thank you.

###

FOR EXERCISE 4

POLICE PRESS RELEASE

At 10:32 p.m., a police officer responded to the Speed-E-Mart, 123 E. Main St., after receiving a 911 call. When officers arrived, they found the store's clerk, later identified as Sam Walther, bleeding from the forehead. In an interview with Walther, officers discerned that 20 minutes earlier, two men entered the store and approached the counter. Both men had bandanas over their noses and mouths and wore sunglasses to hide their faces.

One of the men displayed a handgun, shoved a cloth sack into Walther's hands and demanded that Walther empty the register. Walther began to comply when the man with the gun became impatient and struck him in the face with the gun. Walther lost consciousness and fell behind the counter. When he awoke, he found the register empty and the men gone. He then called 911.

LT. BILLY BERG, OFFICER IN CHARGE

"We arrived to find Mr. Walther in a state of confusion. He had clearly been struck in the head with something and he had been bleeding. The paramedics patched him up but he was still shaken so we are going to keep an eye on him. He was able to tell us what happened and it sounds like two other robberies we had this week at other convenience stores in the city. The suspects in each of the cases displayed a gun and demanded that the cashier fill a cloth sack. That said, this is the first time someone was injured during the robbery, and that concerns us. We don't like to see any crimes, but an escalation of violence is extremely problematic. We don't believe Mr. Walther did anything to antagonize these people."

"We work with gas stations, mini-marts and other similar businesses on how best to handle a situation like this. The biggest thing we tell the workers is that they should always comply and never feel bad about handing over the money. The money is insured and your life isn't worth whatever is in the register. Your boss will understand."

"The suspects did a good job of disguising themselves, as we can only say they're both about 6-foot tall and about 200 pounds. We have no hair color, eye color or race information. In two of the robberies, however, the clerks noted they arrived in a mid-1970s Ford pickup truck that was really beat up. It was white with about 50 overlapping bumper stickers on the tailgate. It also had those tiny spare 'donut' tires on the two front wheels. Other than that, we have no information about these people."

SAM WALTHER, CLERK

"It all happened so fast. This white truck pulls up and these guys get out and I'm not thinking anything of it. All of a sudden, they're at the counter and one of them has a gun in my face. It was the scariest thing I've ever seen. I froze."

"They kept saying, 'Fill the bag,' 'Fill the bag,' and I'm trying to fill the bag but my hands don't feel like they're working, but I'm trying to do this. All of a sudden, the guy with the gun makes a move and everything goes black. I was so happy to wake up, even though my head hurt like crazy. I thought I was dead. I figured he shot me."

"I don't feel good about any of this, but I guess it's a bit better that the police know this is going on and that I'm not the only one who had this happen to them. I don't know what else I could have done, but I'm hoping I never have this happen to me again."

BEYOND BASIC REPORTING: NEWS YOU HAVE TO FIND

REVIEW

1. What are the three types of beats your book lists in this chapter? List an example of each type.

2. When you take on a beat, what are some of the questions the book suggests you should ask your predecessor on the beat?

3. What should you hope to collect from a profile subject during each of the three interviews you conduct?

4. What does FOIA stand for, and what does it and other similar laws do for journalistic watchdogs?

5. When it comes to doing "the big story," what are the five basic questions Jaimi Dowdell recommends that you ask to see if your story will be worth the time it will take to report and write it?

WRITING EXERCISES

1. Your book lists several pros and cons associated with beat reporting. Review these ideas and come up with several other positive and negative aspects associated with this type of beat.

2. Keep a running list of simple things you do or encounter every day, and see how many of them you think might lead to a story. These topics could be as basic as how the city changes the light bulbs in traffic lights or how the city monitors people who "adopt a highway" for beautification. Review your list and select three stories you want to explore more deeply for a news feature, and start finding sources for them. When you are done, pick one of the remaining three and do the story.

3. Unplug from all of your electronic devices for no less than four hours with the intention of finding "hidden" stories.

   - Listen to other people's conversations at the school cafeteria or in line at the coffee shop.
   - Look at various historical markers on your campus and read any postings you find on kiosks or bulletin boards.
   - Sit on a bench and observe people as they move all around you as you seek trends in clothing, transportation or anything else.
   - Come back to class with at least three story ideas you think would be good for news features.
   - Write up a short paragraph as to what you think the story is, why it would matter to your audience and who might make for good sources.

4. **BEAT COVERAGE EXERCISE**

   Select a beat area that interests you and spend at least two weeks exploring the area.

   - Meet with at least three people on your beat who have some stake in what happens in your area. You must interview them to gain information about what matters to them and to garner some potential story ideas.
   - Search through at least one set of documents pertaining to your beat. This can be as simple as looking through the booking log at the police department or as complicated as an open-records request for all travel expenses for the school district.

- Come up with three potential story ideas for your beat. If you are selecting a meeting or a speech, it had better have some high-end value. Profiles, depth stories, trend stories and more are better choices. Keep in mind that the better the idea, the better the story. This should include information on the topic, no fewer than three potential sources (named sources, not "a teacher" or "a city council rep.") and a statement as to why you think this story matters.

5. **BEAT STORY EXERCISE**

Based on the three potential story ideas you located, work with your instructor to determine which one would lead to the best potential story. Conduct the interviews with the individuals you selected as potential sources and finish any necessary research to create the proper background for the piece. Write a story that contains no fewer than three human sources.

6. **PROFILE STORY EXERCISE**

Find a person who interests you and create a personality profile on that individual.

- You will want to ask the person if he or she is interested in working with you before you do too much work, but gather at least a small amount of background research on this individual.

- Follow the pattern outlined in the chapter, in which you interview the subject as well as several people who know that person.

- Conduct enough background research to know what questions need to be asked, and spend enough time with the person to gather observations and anecdotes.

- Then write a story on this person. It should contain quotes and information from the main subject and no fewer than two additional human sources.

7. **NEWS FEATURE STORY EXERCISE**

Find a topic that interests you, and come up with a way to craft a news feature on it. It should have a news peg, but it shouldn't be hard news. For example, a story on how retail clerks deal with people on Black Friday would have a news peg if you wrote it in mid-November, but not in mid-June.

This could be anything from a group of motorcycle riders who love to knit to a profile of a local business that serves coffee and financial advice. The story should have a minimum of three human sources and have broad appeal. Stories like this tend to range from 1,000 to 1,500 words, if you are looking for a word-count target.

8. **OPEN-RECORDS STORY EXERCISE**

Read Appendix C in the back of your book on how to file an open-records request, and review the process. Research a topic that interests you and would involve reporting that could be aided by an open-records request. This could be something like a request for contracts between your school's athletic department and other schools for scheduling games (presuming at least one of the institutions is a public school). It could also be something that interests you on the town, city or county level, such as police reports of domestic violence, the number of traffic tickets doled out by the county sheriff or data pertaining to the number of regulations the city passed each year over the past decade.

Formally request the documents, and then review them for potentially interesting news stories. Examine the data for anomalies, patterns and trends. Interview subjects who have direct ties to the data (people who collect or use the data) as well as people who might be affected by the data (people who get the most parking tickets or people who live in areas affected by a spending plan). Write a story that contains at least two human sources and cites data you received as part of your open-records request.

BROADCAST-STYLE WRITING AND VOICING

REVIEW

1. Your book notes that broadcast writing is done "for the ear." What does that mean, and how do you write in that fashion?

2. What are pace and flow? Why do they matter specifically in broadcast writing?

3. How does an inverted-pyramid lead differ from a broadcast lead? What is it about broadcast journalism that makes this difference necessary?

4. What are the four broadcast story formats discussed in this chapter? Explain each of them in one or two sentences.

5. What does the term "wallpaper" mean in a broadcast context? How can you write a script to avoid this problem?

WRITING EXERCISES

1. Below are words that could easily be mispronounced. Research the terms and write a pronouncer for each of them. Make sure to use hyphens to separate the syllables and capital letters to show emphasis.

   a. Chrysanthemum

   b. Nevada, Missouri

   c. Chutzpah

   d. Ndamukong Suh

   e. Xiphoid

   f. Tsetse fly

   g. Phlegm

   h. Siobhan

2. Find five words or terms you would use locally that you think might be problematic for people outside of your area. These could be names of people and places or abbreviations and acronyms. Write a sentence that includes each word as well as a properly structured pronouncer.

3. Below are sentences that need to be rewritten for broadcast style. Consider using strong noun-verb-object structure, trimming unneeded words and using words that add sound and feel to them as you write for the ear. Also, review the section on numbers, symbols, acronyms and other readability issues so you can apply those suggestions here:

   a. The ground was severely wetted by the 2.8 inches of precipitation that fell near Westfield Beach.

   b. Garbage men and garbage women were collecting bags of trash when the very bad smell led them to the dead woman's body.

c. The St. Louis Cardinals were defeated by the Milwaukee Brewers when Ryan Braun hit a ninth-inning home run very far into the bleachers in right field.

d. Park rangers were told by vacationers that many clusters of bees were flying close to their heads.

e. The city will spend $1,202,005 on a park, or 3.04 times what the park is worth, IRS officials said.

f. James Smith was formally accused in court today of meeting Dr. Wilson Middlebrook at 242 St. Paul St. and shooting him to death.

4. Your book notes the pros and cons of using the term "you" in broadcast journalism. Given your own experiences with viewing broadcast and your own sense of journalism, do you think using second person is effective in this form of writing? Defend your answer.

5. Find a local story that your area television station covered and that your local newspaper covered. Analyze the approach each of them took in telling the story, including the sources used, the amount of information they included and how clearly you felt they presented the content. Also, outline the areas in which you think one form of journalism worked better than the other with regard to storytelling. For example, a story about a fire at a fireworks factory will likely lead to a better broadcast story, due in part to the ability to include a lot of quality visuals and strong audio. However, a story on a budget bill might be better in a newspaper, given the paper's ability to lay out more content in a thorough fashion.

6. **READER SCRIPT PRACTICE**

Here is the information on the fire included earlier in the workbook. Write a 20-second reader in broadcast format. Be sure to include a broadcast-style lead and a solid close. Then, record yourself voicing the reader and listen to the final product. If you find that the recording is too long or you made errors with regard to word choices, go back and edit your copy and revoice the reader. Finally, compare and contrast your final copy from the inverted-pyramid exercise with the reader you completed for this assignment. Be sure to examine length, structure and word choice in your analysis of your work.

Source: Lt. Carl Wexler, Daytonville Fire Department

INFORMATION: The Daytonville Fire Department deployed Ladder Truck 5, Chief's Car 4, Pumper Truck 11 and additional support vehicles to 121 S. Eighth St. after receiving a 911 call around 5:30 p.m. Tuesday. Firefighters arrived to find the two-story, four-bedroom home fully enveloped in flames. The homeowner, Clarence Combs, was outside of the home, as was his wife, Jane, and their daughter, Zelda. He stated that no one else was left inside. Nobody was injured.

Firefighters deployed several hose lines and fought the blaze for three hours until getting full control of the situation. After the fire was extinguished, two fire marshals investigated the scene and determined that the fire was caused by an overheated dryer in the basement. The fire then spread along the basement's ceiling, which consisted mostly of very old wood. The house was constructed in 1892 and was the oldest home in Daytonville.

The home is considered a total loss, and the loss is estimated to be $300,000 in damages.

7. **VO/SOT SCRIPT PRACTICE**

Here is the information you received earlier in the workbook about an armed robbery at a convenience store. Use this information to script a VO/SOT. You can use any of the information here for scripting, but you can also consider the quoted material for potential soundbites. Include at least two soundbites (two from one source or one from each of the two sources). Make sure you can write in and out of your bites effectively. Format your text to mimic the split-screen format in your book. Then, make a list of all of the video you would need to shoot to cover your scripted content. Keep in mind, you want quality b-roll, not wallpaper video.

POLICE PRESS RELEASE

At 10:32 p.m., a police officer responded to the Speed-E-Mart, 123 E. Main St., after receiving a 911 call. When officers arrived, they found the store's clerk, later identified as Sam Walther, bleeding from the forehead. In an interview with Walther, officers discerned that

20 minutes earlier, two men entered the store and approached the counter. Both men had bandanas over their noses and mouths and wore sunglasses to hide their faces.

One of the men displayed a handgun, shoved a cloth sack into Walther's hands and demanded that Walther empty the register. Walther began to comply when the man with the gun became impatient and struck him in the face with the gun. Walther lost consciousness and fell behind the counter. When he awoke, he found the register empty and the men gone. He then called 911.

LT. BILLY BERG, OFFICER IN CHARGE

"We arrived to find Mr. Walther in a state of confusion. He had clearly been struck in the head with something and he had been bleeding. The paramedics patched him up but he was still shaken so we are going to keep an eye on him. He was able to tell us what happened and it sounds like two other robberies we had this week at other convenience stores in the city. The suspects in each of the cases displayed a gun and demanded that the cashier fill a cloth sack. That said, this is the first time someone was injured during the robbery, and that concerns us. We don't like to see any crimes, but an escalation of violence is extremely problematic. We don't believe Mr. Walther did anything to antagonize these people."

"We work with gas stations, mini-marts and other similar businesses on how best to handle a situation like this. The biggest thing we tell the workers is that they should always comply and never feel bad about handing over the money. The money is insured and your life isn't worth whatever is in the register. Your boss will understand."

"The suspects did a good job of disguising themselves, as we can only say they're both about 6-foot tall and about 200 pounds. We have no hair color, eye color or race information. In two of the robberies, however, the clerks noted they arrived in a mid-1970s Ford pickup truck that was really beat up. It was white with about 50 overlapping bumper stickers on the tailgate. It also had those tiny spare 'donut' tires on the two front wheels. Other than that, we have no information about these people."

SAM WALTHER, CLERK

"It all happened so fast. This white truck pulls up and these guys get out and I'm not thinking anything of it. All of a sudden, they're at the counter and one of them has a gun in my face. It was the scariest thing I've ever seen. I froze."

"They kept saying, 'Fill the bag,' 'Fill the bag,' and I'm trying to fill the bag but my hands don't feel like they're working, but I'm trying to do this. All of a sudden, the guy with the gun makes a move and everything goes black. I was so happy to wake up, even though my head hurt like crazy. I thought I was dead. I figured he shot me."

"I don't feel good about any of this, but I guess it's a bit better that the police know this is going on and that I'm not the only one who had this happen to them. I don't know what else I could have done, but I'm hoping I never have this happen to me again."

8. **SCRIPT AND VOICE EXERCISE 1**

Select one of the events you attended for your exercise in Chapter 7 (meeting, speech) and convert your content to a 20-second broadcast reader. Write the script in the proper formatting, and make sure to include pronouncers where necessary. Then, voice the content into a recording device. Feel free to repeat the voicing and edit the script if you aren't satisfied with your work or if it runs too long. You can do this exercise with a new event if you feel it would be more effective that way. You can also repeat this with multiple events or topics.

9. **SCRIPT AND VOICE EXERCISE 2**

    Select a press release from your local police department or fire department website and use it to write a script for a 25-second reader. Write the script in proper formatting, and make sure to include pronouncers where necessary. Then, voice the content into a recording device. Feel free to repeat the voicing and edit the script if you aren't satisfied with your work or if it runs too long. In the case of a police press release, be careful with legal terms pertaining to arrests, convictions and presumption of guilt. Make sure you understand the terms you are using.

COLLECTING AUDIO AND VISUALS IN THE FIELD

REVIEW

1. What are the four types of microphones listed in the chapter, and what purpose does each one serve?

2. What are some of the things you should consider when it comes to selecting a video camera, according to the chapter?

3. What does the term "dead art" mean? What are the four examples of this type of photography listed in the chapter, and why are these kinds of images bad for your storytelling?

4. What is the rule of thirds, and how does it apply to still photography and videography?

WRITING EXERCISES

1. Take the script you wrote for the exercises in Chapter 9 and plan a video shoot to go with it. Determine not only what images and audio you want to capture but also what types of shots you want to get for each segment. (For example, you might determine that you want to capture video at a park for a story about

summer fun for kids. You will want to get a long shot that establishes the scene and several medium shots of kids playing on playground equipment. If your story were on a group of people who build ships in bottles, you will obviously want to plan a large number of close-up shots that provide details.) Also, select sources for potential interviews and plot out some questions you want to ask them so you can get good soundbites.

2. Review an online publication, newspaper or magazine and assess the overall quality of the photography. Examine the visuals in terms of content selection, storytelling and overall value. Also examine the pieces from a more technical aspect:

   • Are the images in focus or blurry?

   • Does the photographer have tight shots, or do the images require a tighter crop? Do the images abide by the rule of thirds?

   • In your analysis, include suggestions to improve the photography in terms of content and value. (You can skip suggestions such as, "Don't use blurry photos.")

3. Record a video interview with someone in a public area. The interview questions and purpose will be somewhat secondary, as the goal is to see how well your video and audio work out. Once you are done with the interview, review your footage for issues noted in the chapter: problematic background noise, intrusive background objects, fuzzy focus, awkward framing and poor vocal recordings. What problems did you encounter in your interview, and how would you rectify them next time you interview someone?

4. Go to a public place with the purpose of listening for ambient sound. Listen for things like birds chirping, kids playing, traffic roaring by and other similar sounds. What could these sounds add to your storytelling? Why do you think they could be valuable as a part of a package? Explain your thoughts.

5. **CAPTION-WRITING PRACTICE**

   Below is a series of images with some information about them. Use this information to construct a two-sentence photo caption for each image following the formula outlined in the chapter:

a. This is a game between Whitberg High in the dark jerseys and Henshaw High in the white jerseys. Number 41 is Billy Manthe, who is getting ready to pass to Chip Collins (number 53). This was the state championship game that Whitberg won 54-51. Manthe had 26 points, 11 rebounds and 14 assists. It was the first time anyone recorded a triple double in the state finals. He was voted the finals MVP. The two people guarding Manthe are Fletcher Davis (left) and Charlie Chalker (right).

b. The two people in the shot are Jane Stey and Robert Elfin. They are software developers for Smith Wexman LLC, a company that is working on a series of apps that allow farmers to better monitor their crops. The apps they are testing on this tablet will allow the farmers to find places in their fields that need more water, have problems with insects and require special fertilizer. Stey said she was showing Elfin the way she fixed one of the problems with the app in this shot. The fix improved the speed at which information loaded onto the screen.

iStock.com/vgajic

c. Buster Jenkins is snuggling his dog, Butler, a mixed breed that he rescued from a local shelter. Jenkins served in the Army for six years, including three years in war-torn Afghanistan. When he came home, he said he suffered from post-traumatic stress disorder, and during a mental-health appointment, his doctor suggested he find a rescue dog as part of his therapy. Jenkins said Butler gave him purpose and helped him as part of his return to civilian life. Jenkins now runs Pups for Grunts, a nonprofit organization that rescues dogs from animal shelters and matches them with returning military personnel. He has matched more than 200 animals with owners over the past three years.

6. **PHOTO EXERCISE**

   Use a still camera to cover a local event that has a variety of aspects and activities, like a local carnival, a 5K run or a charity fundraiser. You want to capture an array of photos both in terms of the types of shots you take as well as the images themselves. Select one or two images that would make for a good newspaper package. Then, select 15 to 20 of the remaining images to create a quality slideshow. Remember that you want to avoid repeating shots between the newspaper package and the slideshow. You also don't want repetitive shots in the slideshow itself. Structure the slideshow so that it tells a story and that the images transition smoothly from shot to shot.

EDITING AUDIO AND VIDEO

REVIEW

1. What are the three main areas your book discusses with regard to problematic video, and how can you identify these problems and fix them?

2. What are the three questions your book tells you to ask when considering if you should use raw video?

3. Explain how a sequence works in telling a story. Give an example of a story you might tell with video editing, and include examples of each type of shot you might include in a particular sequence.

WRITING EXERCISES

1. Watch a broadcast news story on television or online and keep track of the number and types of shots. What shot type was used the most? The least? Which shots did you think were particularly effective and why? Which ones were problematic and why?

2. Take an audio recording you did of a recent interview, either for this class or for a different journalistic purpose, and look for some portions of the recording that might make for good audio bites. Use an audio-editing program to clip two or three soundbites out of the larger audio and save them as individual files. Then, write a few paragraphs on each bite to explain why you selected those bites and how they meet the standards outlined in the chapter (clarity, storytelling etc.).

3. Take a video recording you did of a recent interview, either for the exercise in Chapter 10 or for a different journalistic purpose.

   • Use a video-editing program to clip two or three bites from out of the raw video and save them as individual files.

   • Write a few paragraphs on each bite to explain why you selected those bites and how they meet the standards outlined in the chapter.

   • If you completed Exercise 2 in this workbook, compare and contrast the approach you took to selecting audio bites and the approach you took to selecting these bites.

4. Find a news story online that uses a segment of raw video as part of its storytelling package.

   • Watch the video and assess its overall contribution to the story as a whole.

   • Analyze the size (length of the video) versus value (how important is it to see all the video) as part of your assessment.

   • Also consider the storytelling aspects of the video and its quality. Should the journalists have used this raw video in this way? Justify your answer.

5. **BITES EXERCISE**

   Attend a public event that will likely interest your audience and conduct at least two on-camera interviews with people involved in the event. When you are done interviewing, select at least two soundbites per source that can stand alone or with a simple bit of text and cut them out of the main interview. Post the bites and any accompanying text to the web, as per your professor's instructions.

6. **VO/SOT EXERCISE 1**

   Attend a public event that would likely lead to a hard-news story, such as a meeting or a press conference with the purpose of creating a VO/SOT.

   - Conduct research in advance to determine how best to cover the event, and sketch out a rough draft of your script so you can better plan your shoot.

   - Capture the video at the event, and conduct at least one interview that will yield at least one quality soundbite for your VO/SOT.

   - After the event, fine-tune your script and select your soundbite(s) for the VO/SOT.

   - Voice your script and edit your package. (Remember, each shot of b-roll should last 4 to 6 seconds within a sequence.) The VO/SOT should be 45 to 50 seconds when you are done.

7. **VO/SOT EXERCISE 2**

   Attend a public event that would likely lead to a news feature, such as a local fair or carnival, with the purpose of creating a VO/SOT on the topic. Follow the guidelines listed in Exercise 6 for the completion of your story. Remember the differences between these types of stories when you build your script. Also pay particular attention to the tone of your voice when you read your script to make sure it reflects the tone of the event. (Happy events shouldn't sound like you are giving a eulogy at a funeral and vice versa.)

8. **PACKAGE EXERCISE**

   Use the video you collected for the Chapter 10 exercise to create a package. (If you don't like the way this video turned out, find a new topic that will be beneficial for this exercise.) The package should use a script that pairs well with the video you shot. (Remember, each shot of b-roll should last 4 to 6 seconds within a sequence.) It should also rely on solid sequencing of shots. Include at least two soundbites from your sources, which should range from 8 to 12 seconds each. Work through the process outlined in your book from importing your video through the reviewing of the package for errors. If you need program-specific directions, refer to Appendix D in the book for hints and tips.

LAW AND THE MEDIA

REVIEW

1. What are the freedoms delineated in the First Amendment to the Constitution?

2. According to your book, what is the difference between "free" press or speech and "consequence-free" press or speech?

3. What does the term "reporter's privilege" mean? What questions do courts generally ask to create a balancing test between a legal agency's right to know and a reporter's desire to protect a source?

4. What are sunshine laws, and what value do they have for journalists?

5. What is the difference between a one-party consent rule and a two-party consent rule regarding recording telephone calls? Do some research and find out which rule applies to your state.

WRITING EXERCISES

1. Research the laws of your state pertaining to open records and open meetings. Then, select another state that in some way matters to you (you were born there, it contains a rival school etc.) and research that state's sunshine laws. How are they similar and how do they differ? Which state do you believe provides the greater amount of openness and transparency? Why?

2. Outline the seven key elements your book states are necessary to win a libel suit. Then assess each of the following statements to determine if they meet the standard of libel. Write a few sentences for each one to justify your answer.

   a. A student journalist issues a false and defamatory statement about another student on your campus but states that the information was only sent by Twitter and thus isn't subject to libel laws.

   b. You publish a story about a professor on your campus who has a second job as "Zingo the Clown," where he performs for children's birthday parties. The professor is embarrassed that this information is now known and threatens to sue you.

   c. A promising local band has a gig at the biggest event in the city. The music critic from the local paper writes a scathing review of the band for his weekly "Musical Notes" column. The band subsequently loses several other paying gigs and threatens to sue the writer and the paper for damages.

   d. The student newspaper analyzes records of grades handed out by professors at your university and finds that approximately 1 out of every 15 professors inflates grades. After the story is published, a professor in sociology calls the paper and threatens to sue for libel because of the story.

3. Below is a series of incidents in which the person involved files a lawsuit against you for libel. For each one, state whether you think someone suing you for libel would win. If you think you are safe, cite the specific defense outlined in the chapter that you think protects you.

   a. Bill Jones is convicted of murder in a court of law. You later write a story about an appeal he has filed, and you refer to him as "convicted killer Bill Jones."

   b. In a story about a car crash, you quote a police officer who tells you that the driver of the Honda Civic, Jim Jacoby, was intoxicated when he caused the accident. After further investigation, it turns out the officer was wrong.

   c. During a review of a local band, you write, "The Disco Points should be called 'The Disappoints' because that's all they did at Friday night's concert." The lead singer of the band has filed suit against you.

   d. You overhear two professors on campus talking about a secretary in their office and how she probably steals money from the department. You send out a tweet that states, "Jill Jacobson of the History Dept. steals money." It turns out to be untrue, but you did delete the tweet after only 10 minutes, and you tweeted an apology.

   e. On a "Rate the Professor" website, you post, "If you have the choice of taking Dr. Victor Domo's stats class at Big Name University or eating rat poison, you should eat rat poison because it's probably better for you." Dr. Domo files suit.

4. Below is a series of incidents in which invasion of privacy could apply. For each one, state whether you think you would be protected from invasion of privacy and why you think this is the case.

   a. You are designing a page that doesn't have any photography, so you pull up a photograph from last year's state math championships featuring two local schoolchildren and pair it with a story titled, "Cognitively impaired students get chance to succeed at local school."

b.   You are doing laundry in a public college's laundry room when you notice that the laundry service worker of the Zeta Zeta Zeta sorority is sorting clothing she just washed. She has a list that tells who wears what size undergarments so she can make sure the items get back to the right sorority members. You snap a quick picture of that list and then publish it.

c.   A local parent forms a group called "Smut-free Schools," lobbying before the school board that pornography is the work of the Devil and that certain images in biology textbooks are an affront to all decent people and should be banned. A week later, you stop by a local gas station and see that parent purchasing a half dozen pornographic magazines. You report this in your paper.

5.   Below is a list of actions you might take as a reporter. Which of these do you believe could land you in trouble under the "intrusion" aspect of invasion of privacy? Read each one and make a determination if intrusion is likely to occur, and justify your answer.

a.   You approach a person at a county fair and ask how she is enjoying herself.

b.   You climb over a fence at a local farm to take pictures of the poor conditions in which the animals are living.

c.   You fly a drone over the top of a local teacher's fenced-in yard to see what she is doing on her day off. She is playing with her children on a trampoline. You take several pictures.

d. You take pictures of people eating outside at a sidewalk café.

e. You know the mayor and the city manager tend to chat while in the city hall restroom, so you set up a recording device to catch some news tips.

6. Select one of the following cases that pertains to media and the law. Research the case and provide a basic outline of what the case entailed and what the court ruled. Explain the importance of this case, and explain how it might apply to journalism being conducted today.

   a. *New York Times v. Sullivan* (1964)

   b. *New York Times v. United States* (1971)

   c. *Branzburg v. Hayes* (1972)

   d. *Nebraska Press Association v. Stuart* (1976)

   e. *Hazelwood v. Kuhlmeier* (1988)

   f. *Hustler Magazine v. Falwell* (1988)

   g. *Gordon v. Love* (2016)

ETHICS

REVIEW

1. What does it mean to be compassionate as part of being an ethical journalist? What are some suggestions your book gives you with regard to this aspect of ethics?

2. What are the three items your book lists as components of the honesty standard? Which of these do you feel is the hardest to achieve as a journalist?

3. In the section on fairness, the book quotes journalist Christiane Amanpour, who notes, "I believe in being truthful, not neutral." What did she mean by this?

WRITING EXERCISES

1. Of the five ethical paradigms listed in the chapter, which one do you feel best fits your own approach to ethics? Explain why this one fits you best and how you use the tenets of it to deal with ethical situations in everyday life. Look at the remaining ethical philosophies and think about which one best fits someone with whom you have the greatest ethical divide. What is it about that person and his or her approach to ethics that rubs you the wrong way?

2. Accuracy is mentioned throughout the book as the dominant value in journalism. Explain how it applies to ethical behavior, drawing from examples listed in the journalism codes of ethics listed in the chapter. What makes accuracy an issue of ethics? How do issues like fairness and comprehensive representation play into this area of ethics?

3. Which of the areas listed in this chapter (honesty, accuracy, diversity, compassion, independence and accountability) do you feel is most important in terms of ethical journalistic behavior? Which area is least important? Explain the rationale behind your choices.

4. Review Andrew Seaman's comments in the chapter regarding the revisions to the SPJ ethical code. He speaks at length about the importance of media literacy and the issues that arose as part of digital proliferation. Given the way in which journalists aren't the only people putting information out on digital platforms, how important do you think the issue of media literacy is for readers and viewers of content? How difficult is it for you as a journalist to see "successful" sites that pander to opinions and bend the truth, knowing that you need to hold yourself to a higher journalistic standard?

5. Below are several scenarios in which the standard of independence comes into play. Review each one and write a short response to explain what you would do in each case and why.

    a. A local merchant is selling a "must-have toy" that parents are lining up around the block to get each time a shipment arrives. Even your own family members are obsessed with getting one of these toys. You ask the merchant if he can tell you when he's getting a new shipment so you can go to the store and report on the chaos.

    He calls you one afternoon and invites you over before he alerts the public about the shipment so you can do some interviewing of store employees before the event. Just before he lets everyone else know about the shipment, he offers you the chance to buy one or two. Do you buy the toy?

b. You are working on a story about a bank robbery, and the police are not releasing the name of the man who was arrested on suspicion of robbing the bank. You receive a phone call from your neighbor, with whom you have had several unpleasant encounters, mostly due to his son playing music too loudly or leaving garbage on your lawn.

He says he knows you work at the local TV station and that your colleagues are probably working on a bank robbery story. "Look," he says. "I know we have a lot of disagreements, but I'm begging you not to put my son's name on TV as the robber. He's a good kid who made a dumb mistake. He even called me from jail to ask me to ask you for forgiveness and mercy." Given that this is your only source of information for the name, do you run the name of the son as the robber?

c. Consider the same scenario as above, but imagine the person calling you for help were your best friend or a close family member. Would you run the name then?

d. You are a photographer who is assigned to cover the state high school track championship. The main story everyone wants to know about is a student from the local high school who lost his brother to cancer one day before the tournament. In a major upset, the student wins the 100-meter dash, setting a state record. In celebration, he runs to the stands, grabs a framed photo of his brother and does a victory lap, holding the photo aloft.

Unfortunately for you, traffic was horrible and you missed the whole thing. The student knows you from your previous work and offers to take another lap with the photo so you can shoot the photo of him. Since no other news outlet had covered the event, no one will ever know that you weren't there on time, and he promises not to tell anyone. What do you do?

e. A senator from your state is likely to face a fierce reelection campaign this year, as a formidable challenger from an opposition party has emerged. The senator has spent the past two years working on various projects with underprivileged students throughout the state and will likely make this a big part of his push for his campaign.

The senator contacts your news outlet and asks if you would be interested in going on a two-week junket throughout the state, where he will visit these areas and check in on all of his ongoing projects. The campaign will pay all of your expenses, such as hotel and food costs, and you will have complete access to the senator and anyone else involved with those projects. Your boss has always left decisions like this up to the individual reporter. What would you do?

6. Review several stories published in a media outlet of your choosing for elements of diversity. Is diversity present or absent in this coverage? How is it emphasized in a positive or negative fashion? Do you see elements of stereotyping? What are they and how could they be avoided?

7. Read the article the New York Times published in the wake of the Jayson Blair fabrication and plagiarism scandal (available at http://www.nytimes.com/2003/05/11/us/correcting-the-record-times-reporter-who-resigned-leaves-long-trail-of-deception.html). Apply the principle of accountability to this piece. Do you think the Times did enough to correct the record? Did the paper acknowledge its errors to your satisfaction? Did the story serve the public, or was it, as some people have argued, an attempt to preserve the paper's own interests? Explain your thoughts.

ANSWER KEY

CHAPTER 1 AUDIENCE-CENTRIC JOURNALISM

1. What is audience-centric journalism? How is it similar to what traditional media outlets have done in years past, and how is it different?

    It puts audience interests at the forefront of reporting and writing, in terms of what information is available, when it is produced and on which platforms the content is provided.

    Answers will vary on similarity/differences.

2. This chapter noted that generations of journalists were previously taught in "silos" based on the fields they saw themselves entering. What does this mean?

    This means that journalists were traditionally trained in one area of the field, such as print or broadcast, and worked only in those areas as opposed to working across platforms or areas.

3. Define and differentiate between audience "wants" and audience "needs" when it comes to a media diet. How does the book say you should balance these topics as a journalist?

    Wants are things we desire because they amuse or entertain us. Needs are things that are good for us that we should have whether we want them or not. The book says that you want to balance entertaining stories with crucial content as well as look for ways to make important stories more engaging for readers.

4. Define and differentiate among the three ways in which the book states you should break down an audience: demographic information, psychographic information and geographic information.

    Demographic information includes measurable items like age and education as well as check-box items such as gender and race. Psychographic information includes personality traits, values and interests, such as interest in sports, the importance one places on local politics and the views people have on issues like gun control or abortion. Geographic information relates to where something happens, with the idea that people are more interested in things happening near them or in areas in which they have a direct attachment.

5. What do the letters in the acronym "FOCII" stand for, and what does it mean overall as a concept?

Fame, oddity, conflict, immediacy and impact. These are the interest elements journalists can emphasize in their stories to appeal to audience members.

CHAPTER 2 CRITICAL THINKING

1. Define critical thinking and give an example of critical versus uncritical thinking.

The Foundation for Critical Thinking defines critical thinking as the art of analyzing and evaluating thought with a view to improving it. Examples will vary.

2. Define and differentiate between learning and thinking.

Learning can involve the memorization of information as well as retaining content that is important. Thinking will involve more broad analysis of content in terms of value and purpose. In short, learning captures the who, what, when and where. Thinking digs into the how and why.

3. What are the four things the book notes are the signs of a good critical thinker?

Raises vital questions and problems by coming to grips with the topic; gathers and assesses relevant information; thinks open-mindedly within alternative systems of thought, recognizing and assessing as need be his or her assumptions, implications and practical consequences; communicates effectively with others in figuring out solutions to complex problems.

4. The chapter notes that you should "avoid self-importance." What does that mean, and how does the chapter suggest you do this?

This means you should keep your ego in check, avoid believing that what you think matters most and put the focus back on your readers. You can do this by thinking of yourself as a conduit of information (or a "frame") for your readers instead of the main attraction for your readers.

CHAPTER 3 BASICS OF WRITING

1. What does your book say are the two most important questions you should consider when you decide how to structure your story?

What matters most? How does this affect me as a reader?

2. The book suggests building a lead from the inside out. What are the two or three key elements that should be at the core of a good lead sentence?

Noun, verb and [direct] object

3. Define and differentiate between a name-recognition lead and an interesting-action lead. How does each lead work, and when is it most appropriate to use each lead?

    A name-recognition lead relies on the element of fame to draw people's attention to a story. An interesting-action lead works better when the "what" matters more than the "who" in a story.

4. How should you order information in your story if you are using the inverted-pyramid format?

    In descending order of importance: from the most important information to the least important information.

5. According to the book, how long should most of your paragraphs be in a standard inverted-pyramid story?

    One sentence per paragraph.

6. Define and differentiate between a direct quote and an indirect quote (also known as paraphrase). What is the purpose and value of each form of quoting? When is it best to use each kind of quote?

    Direct quotes are word-for-word content taken directly from a source and placed between quote marks. Indirect quotes are based on what the source had to say but are rewritten to improve structure, grammar and clarity.

    Examples will vary.

7. What is an attribution, and how does it help you as a journalist?

    An attribution tells your reader who told you the information in the story. This lets readers judge for themselves how credible they believe the information to be based on its source.

8. What is the preferred verb of attribution? What other verbs of attribution are acceptable, and under what circumstances are those verbs acceptable?

    "Said" is the preferred verb. Others include "testified" for court cases, "stated" for documents, "announced" for formal proclamations, "asked" for questions and "according to" to provide variation (use it sparingly).

CHAPTER 4 EXPANDED WRITING

1. What are the three things your book lists as potential bridge elements for your story? When should you use each of the bridge types?

    Lead-cleanup bridge: fills in some missing details from the lead, such as any of the 5W's and 1H.

    Quote bridge: uses the source's own words to clarify the theme and solidify the lead.

Advance-the-story bridge: essentially relies on the standard inverted-pyramid idea of placing the second most important thing second.

2. What are the two ways the book recommends to close a story? When should you use each closing type?

   Closing quote or a wrap-up paragraph. Answers will vary.

3. How does the "kabob" approach to narrative writing work?

   It uses a narrative thread or exemplar related to the story that weaves through several larger categorical topics. This helps provide an individual's story as a microcosm of the bigger issue.

4. What is a nut graph, and what purpose does it serve?

   A nut graph is similar to an inverted-pyramid lead in that it helps readers understand why a narrative story has relevance and value to them.

5. Define and differentiate between linear and nonlinear storytelling. Outline the benefits and drawbacks of each.

   Linear storytelling moves from the front of the story to the end of the story in a straight-ahead fashion, much like a newspaper or magazine story.

   Nonlinear storytelling is more like a web of content in which readers can select the order in which they consume content.

   Benefits and drawbacks will vary.

CHAPTER 5 SOCIAL MEDIA

1. What are some of the hints online marketing guru John Rampton offers for building a social media audience? Of the items listed in the chapter, which one do you think is most important? Why?

   Identify goals and objectives, let them know you are human, understand their needs, produce valuable content, consistently post at a comfortable rate.

   Choices will vary.

2. What are the suggestions the chapter offers you for how to use Twitter as a reporter? Which suggestion mirrors an approach you are already taking on social media? Which suggestion gave you a new idea to try?

   Use noun-verb-object structure, tweet to be read, use proper spelling and grammar, keep an audience-centric focus, be careful with the tweets of others.

   Responses will vary.

3. What is a blog? How is it similar to and different from traditional mass media such as newspapers or magazines?

The term is the shortened version of "web log." Blogs use a diary-style approach to providing content on niche topics of interest for writers.

Responses will vary.

4. What are the three suggestions your book offers you for how best to use social media for your audience? Which of the three do you think is most important? Why?

    Content is king, use the right tool for the right job and less is more.

    Responses will vary.

CHAPTER 6 INTERVIEWING

1. What are the three crucial questions your book lists with regard to critically thinking about an interview's purpose? How does each of them affect your approach to an interview?

    Who is this person? What value does the source have for the story? How badly do I need this source?

    Impact statements will vary.

2. What are the pros and cons of an email interview? When should you use them, and when should you avoid them?

    Pros: quick access for simple answers, ready-made transcripts and sources like it.

    Cons: weaker reporting opportunities, and you don't bond with your source. Use them when you have no other options or you just need simple answers.

    Avoid them when you need a deeper, broader interview or to establish trust with a source.

3. What is a loaded question, and why is it bad?

    A loaded question is one that includes assumptions or statements that unfairly corner a source.

4. When you contact someone to set up an interview, what should you tell this person about you and your needs relating to that interview?

    Who you are, what your story is about, why you think the person has value as a source, what your deadline is and how much time you will need for the interview.

5. What is the primary difference between an open-ended question and a closed-ended question? When is it appropriate to use each of them?

    Closed-ended questions lead to simple yes/no or multiple-choice answers. They tend to be questions about the "who, what, where and when" aspects of a story.

    Open-ended questions seek longer, more elaborative answers. They tend to be questions about the "how" and "why" aspects of a story.

6. According to your book, about how many prepared questions should you have for a standard news interview?

   Four or five.

CHAPTER 7 BASIC REPORTING

1. In preparing for a basic reporting assignment, what are some sources you should use to research the event?

   Previous stories, source documents, official websites.

2. Your book mentions that you should "be sure you are sure" when it comes to basic facts. What are some of the things the chapter says you should do to keep inaccuracies out of your copy?

   Check spelling, review proper nouns, look at numbers and review the math.

3. What are the three types of nonsporting events your book notes that you will likely cover as a beginning reporter? How are they similar? How are they different?

   Meetings, speeches and news conferences.

   Responses will vary.

4. What are the key items you should include in a story about a sporting event?

   The score, the atmosphere, the records, the history or rivalry aspects, statistics and injuries.

5. What are the two pieces of advice your book offers when it comes to covering a crime or disaster?

   Stay calm and stay safe.

6. What are the key items you should include in a crime or disaster story?

   Any death or severity of injuries, damage amounts, identities of people involved in the incident and what happened during the event.

CHAPTER 8 BEYOND BASIC REPORTING

1. What are the three types of beats your book lists in this chapter? List an example of each type.

   Thematic beats: police and fire, city government etc.

   Geographic beats: coverage of rural areas, certain neighborhoods etc.

   Conceptual beats: multiculturalism

2. When you take on a beat, what are some of the questions the book suggests you should ask your predecessor on the beat?

What big stories are coming down the road? What stories need extra work or should be followed up? Do you have any "I wish I had gotten to that" topics you think are really valuable? What were some of the most problematic parts of the beat? Which people were really helpful sources? Which ones made you wish you never took this job? Where should I spend most of my time, both physically and in terms of coverage?

3. What should you hope to collect from a profile subject during each of the three interviews you conduct?

   First interview should collect basic information about the source as well as other potential sources for the profile.

   Second interview should follow up with new information from the sources you interviewed since the first interview, clear up discrepancies and gather some observations.

   Third interview should be primarily to gather observations, feel and depth.

4. What does FOIA stand for, and what does it and other similar laws do for journalistic watchdogs?

   Freedom of Information Act. These laws allow the citizenry to have access to documents and meetings of public figures in order to improve democracy and create transparency in government.

5. When it comes to doing "the big story," what are the five basic questions Jaimi Dowdell recommends that you ask to see if your story will be worth the time it will take to report and write it?

   Does this story answer a question? Does the story break new ground? Does the story have potential for impact? Are there victims or does this affect people? Does this have a point to it?

CHAPTER 9 BROADCAST WRITING AND VOICING

1. Your book notes that broadcast writing is done "for the ear." What does that mean, and how do you write in that fashion?

   It means you should write copy so people can understand it when they hear it. You should write in short sentences, use common words and include words that have sounds built into them.

2. What are pace and flow? Why do they matter specifically in broadcast writing?

   Pace is the speed at which you can read through a piece. Tighter sentences quicken the pace, while longer sentences slow it down.

   Flow is how smoothly a script moves from point to point in the story.

These matter because the proper pace and flow can lead to a fluid and smooth read for the journalists and a much better experience for the audience.

3. How does an inverted-pyramid lead differ from a broadcast lead? What is it about broadcast journalism that makes this difference necessary?

    A broadcast lead is akin to a headline in print, in that it gets the audience members' attention before giving them the important details. Broadcast journalism does this because viewers are often distracted or busy while the news is on, so the lead needs to grab their attention first and then proceed with the story.

4. What are the four broadcast story formats discussed in this chapter? Explain each of them in one or two sentences.

    Reader: The simplest piece that has the journalist simply reading the copy to the audience without video.

    VO: Stands for voice-over and has the journalist reading the copy while video pertaining to the story plays.

    VO/SOT (Voice-over/sound on tape): This is an advanced version of the VO, in that it incorporates at least one soundbite.

    Package: A traditional news story that includes the reporter's voice, b-roll, sound bites and even a standup.

5. What does the term "wallpaper" mean in a broadcast context? How can you write a script to avoid this problem?

    Wallpaper describes video that lacks storytelling value but is used to cover over the reporter's voice during a story. It can include random crowd shots or building shots. You can avoid this by writing script copy that matches better with what video you have available.

CHAPTER 10 COLLECTING AUDIO AND VISUALS

1. What are the four types of microphones listed in the chapter, and what purpose does each one serve?

    Built-in mic: Comes with the device and is always there for you.

    Stick mic: Used for interviews and can gather other directional sound.

    Lavalier mic: Good for interviews as they are unobtrusive but can be easily broken, and they pick up any movement your source makes.

    Boom mic: This allows you to gather sound from a distance by extending the boom pole.

2. What are some of the things you should consider when it comes to selecting a video camera, according to the chapter?

   What is your goal? What recording format do you want? What are your sound options? What accessories matter to you?

3. What does the term "dead art" mean? What are the four examples of this type of photography listed in the chapter, and why are these kinds of images bad for your storytelling?

   Dead-art photos are images that lack people or natural action and reaction. Examples include photos of buildings, posed photos, group art and mug shots.

4. What is the rule of thirds, and how does it apply to still photography and videography?

   The rule of thirds notes that you should not center the subject of your image in the frame. Instead, you should place the action or focal point of your shot on the four points of the frame created by the intersection of tic-tac-toe lines you mentally overlay onto the image. This improves readability for your audience and keeps their attention on the most important elements of the image.

CHAPTER 11 EDITING AUDIO AND VIDEO

1. What are the three main areas your book discusses with regard to problematic video, and how can you identify these problems and fix them?

   Unstable images, awkward framing and poor focus. Fixes will vary.

2. What are the three questions your book tells you to ask when considering if you should use raw video?

   Will someone watch this? Is it boring? Does it tell a story?

3. Explain how a sequence works in telling a story. Give an example of a story you might tell with video editing, and include examples of each type of shot you might include in a particular sequence.

   A sequence allows a viewer to progress through a scene as the reporter discusses the story. Example: A long shot can establish a class full of students, a medium shot can show a student typing on a laptop and a close-up shot can zoom in on her fingers typing on the keyboard.

CHAPTER 12 LAW AND MEDIA

1. What are the freedoms delineated in the First Amendment to the Constitution?

   Press, speech, assembly, petition and religion.

2. According to your book, what is the difference between "free" press or speech and "consequence-free" press or speech?

   Free speech under the Constitution means only that the government cannot prevent you from publishing content or speaking out. It does not mean there will not be consequences for your actions, such as the private business you work for firing you as a result of your actions or someone suing you for libel.

3. What does the term "reporter's privilege" mean? What questions do courts generally ask to create a balancing test between a legal agency's right to know and a reporter's desire to protect a source?

   This pertains to a reporter's ability to protect confidential sources. The courts generally ask if the person subpoenaing the journalist tried all other reasonable ways to get the information, if the reporter possesses crucial information or if the subpoena is a fishing expedition and if the public has an overriding public interest in the information.

4. What are sunshine laws, and what value do they have for journalists?

   These are rules and laws that dictate how public business must be conducted and public documents must be accessible. These laws allow journalists to examine the actions of public officials so they can provide this information to the public.

5. What is the difference between a one-party consent rule and a two-party consent rule regarding recording telephone calls? Do some research and find out which rule applies to your state.

   One-party consent means that it is legal for a person to record a telephone call without telling the other person on the line that the call is being recorded.

   Two-party consent means that both participants in the call are legally required to know the call is being recorded.

   Answers will vary.

CHAPTER 13 ETHICS

1. What does it mean to be compassionate as part of being an ethical journalist? What are some suggestions your book gives you with regard to this aspect of ethics?

   Answers will vary on rationale. Suggestions: Think before you act. Be human.

2. What are the three items your book lists as components of the honesty standard? Which of these do you feel is the hardest to achieve as a journalist?

   Be upfront in your reporting. Keep your promises. Be fair. Answers will vary.

3. In the section on fairness, the book quotes journalist Christiane Amanpour, who notes, "I believe in being truthful, not neutral." What did she mean by this?

   Neutrality is providing equal coverage, regardless of its accuracy. Truthfulness is about remaining honest and accurate in coverage while remaining fair in your reporting.